The Art of Coarse Bridge

By the same author

The Art of Coarse Cricket
The Art of Coarse Gardening
The Art of Coarse Cookery
The Art of Coarse Entertaining
The Art of Coarse Language

The Art of Coarse Bridge

Spike Hughes

Illustrated by John Jensen

HUTCHINSON OF LONDON

Hutchinson & Co (Publishers) Ltd
3 Fitzroy Square, London W1

London Melbourne Sydney Auckland
Wellington Johannesburg and agencies
throughout the world

First published August 1970
Second impression December 1972
Third impression June 1976
© Spike Hughes 1970
Illustrations © Hutchinson & Co
(Publishers) Ltd 1970

Printed in Great Britain by litho by The Anchor Press Ltd
and bound by Wm Brendon & Son Ltd
both of Tiptree, Essex

ISBN 0 09 102750 0

*To Charmian
and our partners and opponents
pictured within*

FERNANDO: Here's my hand

MIRANDA: And mine with my heart in't

Contents

1 First Principles

HAVING failed to convince you that it is anything but a reckless game of chance, the evangelists of bridge will insist that at any rate it is a social asset.

Well, that depends very much on the sort of company you keep and why you ever took up bridge in the first place. There may, of course, be some who regard bridge as a social asset—in the kind of society, for instance, where there is nothing odd about spending an evening with three people whom you want to talk to so little that you have to play bridge with them to ensure that there is no conversation. But, for most people, if there is one thing more than another that interferes with a social occasion, disrupting congenial talk and bringing the lingering coda of a good meal to a premature end, it is bridge.

There are, nevertheless, a great many who like nothing better than to spend an evening with three people all of whom want to enjoy congenial talk and play bridge at the same time. It is to them that this study is addressed.

You may perhaps have noticed that I referred above to 'taking up' bridge. This is to distinguish the game played by Us from that played by Them (who have actually had lessons in the game with the avowed object of winning money or money's worth, and—of course—of acquiring a social asset).

People take up bridge for an infinite variety of reasons: sometimes under the influence of heredity or environment; sometimes out of curiosity; sometimes as an escape from

the boredom of routine, which is what happened during
the last war when the increased sophistication of enlisted
personnel led to bridge almost entirely supplanting the
traditional solo whist and ha'penny nap of an earlier
generation of Other Ranks; and sometimes as a desperate
means of sheer self-defence.

This was my own experience. I was literally talked into
it by a quartet of people whose regular nightly noisy
chatter, before, during and after every hand of family
bridge, made it absolutely impossible for a non-participant
like myself to read or even doze off in another part of the
same room. When they were short of a fourth they
listened to Wagner on the gramophone, which for a
non-Wagnerian non-participant like myself was even
worse.

It wasn't just the chatter that was distracting, but the
nonsensical baby-talk it consisted of. Words like 'singleton'
(or 'simpleton', was it?) and 'doubleton', 'ruff' and
'finesse' and 'Yarborough' were gibberish compared
with the few ritual phrases I was used to at the card
table—like 'stick' and 'twist' and 'buy one'; these were
part of the limited vocabulary needed to play the
direct, no-messing-about-and-pretending-there's-any-skill-
in-it game of vingt-et-un, whose practice I learned as a
child from a nineteenth-century volume called *Sports and
Pastimes for the Young*.

The noise created by the post-mortem wrangling and
recrimination which regularly followed every hand of
this 'family' bridge was worse than snap. On the principle
that the best form of defence is attack, and that if you
can't beat 'em, join 'em, I finally abandoned my seat in
the corner of the room and took up the game which had
been such a disturbing element in my pursuit of personal
peace and quiet after dinner.

I found myself in some pretty mixed company. It included a lady who would never play unless she sat on her handkerchief, and her husband who insisted that even beginners (in fact particularly beginners) should play for money, if only for a halfpenny a hundred. The aim of this, he argued, was to curb reckless bidding and doubling; it did nothing of the sort, of course. The accident of losing 1s. 5d. old style ($£$0·071 new style), by going six down, vulnerable, doubled and redoubled, never deterred or discouraged the determined beginner: it merely added to the husband's already ample fortune, or (if you happened to be his partner) affected his blood pressure so much that you only hoped he had made an intelligible will in time.

The fact that money entered into the very first stages of taking up bridge confirmed once and for all that bridge is a gambling game. Nobody backs horses without betting with money, or plays roulette for tiddlywink counters. There would be no point. It is the same with bridge. Of course, if you win on the horses that is due to your knowledge of form; if you win at roulette that is due to your private and personal system; if you win at bridge it is entirely due to your skill and experience. That is not gambling. It is only gambling if you lose—as who doesn't?

This is not to say that skill does not enter into bridge to a certain extent. At bridge, unlike other gambling games, once you have thrown your dice, as it were, you have not altogether lost control over what you've put your money on. At the races or at the Casino once you've backed your horse or your number there is nothing you can do to influence the behaviour of the horse or the roulette wheel and so affect the fate of your money.

But with bridge it is often possible with a small slam that is rightly 'never there' to lose less money on the hand than you ought to have done. And if you can't do this by brilliant play you may at least be able to cause idiotic play on your opponents' part by distracting their attention, making them drunk, or provoking them to quarrel among themselves.

It will be obvious from this, I think, that one of the first principles of Coarse Bridge is to choose as your table companions players who, if not reckless gamblers, at least accept that an odd five hundred points won or lost here or there are of little consequence, and can be explained away in the good-humoured give-and-take, thrust-and-parry of the general debate which inevitably takes place immediately the hand is finished, if not actually before. In short, it is not the winning or the losing, but the playing of the game that matters.

Apart from anything else, over-eagerness to win, or to retrieve one's losses, can result in extending play far beyond sensible time limits, and an otherwise enjoyable evening can deteriorate into an exhausting experience. Mind you, this can also happen—and very often does— when the sole object of continuing to play is not to win for the sake of prestige, or of adjusting the balance of payments, but to finish a rubber that has been game-all for the past hour and a half with nobody having the skill or the cards to deal (literally) the *coup de grâce*. At this stage neither you nor your opponents care who wins the rubber so long as the game can be brought to an overdue end and everybody can go to bed.

The commonest cause of the endless final rubber is a commendable desire on the part of both pairs of players to finish the evening in style with a slam. This kind of spectacular finale happens far more often than one might expect, but it takes an awful lot of scoring above the line before anyone actually has—as distinct from imagining they have—the right cards to do it with.

There are times, however, when the prolongation of the unending final rubber is due to the determination of one player at the table who, instead of throwing in his hand when everybody else does, opens fourth in hand with the sort of cards you ought to go misère on. He will bid an optimistic One Club which everybody passes, and then go three down. He isn't doubled because his opponents are too sleepy to think of it, and in any case he couldn't have been doubled into game. If there were a chance of doubling him into game, of course, his opponents would most certainly wake up and take it—as a desperate means of ending the rubber and so being able to go home to bed.

The appearance at the table of one of these Last-Ditch Drakes (so-called because they *must* finish their game first) always tends to come as a surprise. It is a part that can be played by a man or a woman, and is often played by somebody who, rather puzzlingly, has never acted that way before—at least not in all the years you have been playing with them. Because of the unexpectedness of the situation it is virtually impossible to guard against it by not inviting known offenders to play. Not only impossible, but unwise. If you carried on like that you'd never get a game yourself in your own house. The only thing to do is to trust that—since bridge is known to be a game of chance—the cards will be better this time, and not to black-list anybody.

Above all, Coarse Bridge is a game for the player not the spectator. The rawest set of beginners can get more satisfaction out of it than any comparable four players can derive from, for instance, that other great Social Asset (with tea), lawn tennis. Unless all the players can get the ball over the net and then keep it in play, there is no pleasure in lawn tennis for anyone. In the extreme case,

The 'Last-Ditch Drake'

each player invariably loses his service by a series of four double faults, the first set is interminable and the score can reach 100 games all before night falls and mercifully interrupts the proceedings.

But those who take up bridge need suffer none of this frustration. Thirteen tricks are played, and whatever the result at the end of what may be the first hand that any of those at the table have played in their lives, everybody feels that something positive is going on. And since you are playing a game of chance, the odds are great that the cards will fall so that nobody can help winning a game sooner or later—even if it is achieved in cautious stages of One-Club-bid-and-made at a time.

Finally, it is in the nature of things that Coarse Bridge is generally played in the evening. This is firstly because not enough players ever seem to have an afternoon off to make up a four; secondly, when they do—which is on Sunday—they prefer to put their feet up and fall asleep over bridge articles in the Sunday papers, and so refresh themselves for the strenuous rubbers to come.

This practice of playing only in the evening is responsible for one of the most prominent and important features of Coarse Bridge. It enables the hostess to spend the afternoon in the kitchen preparing a meal which will be worthy of you when you come to dinner and cards like the cultured and civilised gambler you are.

2 *Organisation*

Formez vos bataillons!
ROUGET DE LISLE

ACCORDING to the Laws of Bridge, as laid down by Crockford's (the gambling club, not the Church of England's *Clerical Directory*), it has been . . .
Correction. I seem to have been misinformed.

> *For:* 'as laid down by Crockford's, etc.'
> *Read:* 'as determined by the Portland Club, the European Bridge League and the National Laws Commission of America'.

Anyway, these three imposing bodies, and probably Crockford's as well, have determined that Contract Bridge, like Auction Bridge and whist before it, 'is a game for four, two partnerships of two opposing each other. The partners sit facing each other.'

While the laws of Coarse Bridge observe the basic principles of the number and disposal of players required for a game, it is unwise to presume that because you have four players they are going to be enough, not merely to make up a table, but to keep the game going to the end.

I do not suggest by this that a number of substitutes should sit on the sidelines to take the place of players who might receive injuries at the table inflicted on them by

well-aimed kicks from their partners (for at bridge, unlike
other violent games, such as football or hockey, injuries
are received from your own side, not your opponents).
The purpose of arranging that at least five people are
available to take the field is to ensure that when the time
comes the hostess does not have to depend on her chance
of being dummy to be able to go out into the kitchen
and put on the potatoes. A fifth player, preferably the
hostess's husband who has been in his study all this time
writing a book (of a sort) about bridge (of a sort), can
take over to relieve the cook so that she is free to put on
the potatoes without risk of holding up the game, and
—more important—to take them off when they are
done.

It is obviously better to choose your fifth player from
the home ground, but it is possible to invite what one
might call 'natural No. 5's'—players who are good
company at the dinner table and quite happy to retire
from the game from time to time and read the copies of
the *New Yorker* that have arrived since they were last
invited. Such players are invaluable when the other
guests are a generation younger than you are and have
the stamina to go on playing until long past your bedtime.
The invited natural No. 5 can take the hostess's place
before she falls asleep over her cards, or else he can take
the host's place if the host isn't lasting the pace so well as
his wife, which is likely.

Considering that there are already two of you pleased
to provide an evening of dinner and bridge in your own
house, it really ought to be easy enough to find another
couple to make up a four. In practice this is far from being
the case. To be on the safe side, if you want to be sure of
two players you must invite three. If all three turn up, the
odd one out will not want for a game, for, as I have shown,

a good No. 5 will always find a seat at the table. And the husband can always be sent out to get on with his work.

To make doubly sure, you should invite four players (making six altogether, including yourselves), as it is by no means unusual for two of the three originally selected guests to cry off. This is an occurrence common to all Coarse Bridge circles, but the reasons for it vary according to where you live and what your friends do for a living. In our own neighbourhood, where we draw for our players on a number of friends who work in one capacity or another at our local opera house, such last-minute hazards as an extra lighting rehearsal, or an emergency understudy call, can lead to a change in our cast involving up to four characters. When this happens you have to start telephoning around for help from somebody not so entangled with the Muses.

One of the most satisfying features of organising an evening of Coarse Bridge is that nobody ever forgets the date of a fixture. If they do not turn up it is not because they have forgotten but because they are unable to keep the appointment, and they will always give you adequate warning.

From time to time my wife, whose bridge is orthodox and indeed expert enough for her to get invited out to rather a higher class of bridge than she's used to at home, finds herself in the company of players with diaries. These are produced at the end of the afternoon's play with a general expectant cry, 'Now, when shall we do this again?'

My wife has a diary, but seldom remembers to take it out with her; when she does it presents an intriguing contrast to the diaries consulted by the rest of the company

—diaries bound in morocco, and elegant with gold initials and gold-topped pencils. Charmian's diary is bound in plastic and comes to her with the compliments of her bookmaker. Even when she does remember to take it with her, she never writes in it. This is because the dates suggested for 'doing this again' are so far ahead—two months, three months, six months sometimes—that she can have no possible idea whether she will even be in England at that time. All that she can be sure of is that, according to her diary and unless the courses are waterlogged, there will be racing on that particular Monday at Doncaster, Chepstow, Leicester, Redcar, Sandown Park, Uttoxeter, Wetherby, Cartmel, Devon and Exeter, Hexham, Towcester, Fakenham, Fontwell Park, Hereford and Huntingdon. Perhaps somebody would telephone her nearer the time?

Forgetting to take a diary out to a bridge party is one well-ingrained streak of Coarse Bridge behaviour that must come out in all who have ever played that form of the game. Coarse Bridge fixtures are not put down in diaries; they are made over the telephone about two days before they take place—or less, if there is no catering problem. The efficiency of the method is such that the inexperienced, and therefore still over-cautious, organiser who asks seven people just to make sure, can well find himself on the night with two tables of bridge to cope with. This demands the sort of improvisation at which all organisers have to be instinctively adept; if they aren't, they had better pack up and be an organisee.

On the first, and so far the only, occasion when I was involved as a guest in a case of this kind of over-booking (a process in which man is almost as expert as the computer, but not quite), Rex, by no means an inexperienced or over-cautious organiser, had improvised well; there was no shortage of food, drink, tables, chairs, equipment or convivial atmosphere.

The only trouble was that, owing to a shortage of elbow room in a bachelor's drawing room, the players were inclined to base their bids on what they heard coming from the other closely placed table. An opening of One Diamond by South at Table I would be answered by North at Table II with Two Clubs, which, taken by his partner to be a Strong-Two opening, would be denied by Two Diamonds. This kind of cross-talk, with people at one table using the Blackwood 4–5 No Trump convention and discovering from people at the next that they had no Aces at all, led to some bizarre results. But in spite of the confusion—or more likely because of it—the final rubber at each table ended spectacularly with a slam, which in one case rightly helped towards reimbursing the host for his trouble and hospitality.

Coarse Bridge festivals like this do not happen often, of course. Expense and space are too often against it, but as an occasional experience it is definitely exhilarating and gives everybody an exalted feeling of extravagance and showing off, of masquerading as Bridge Gentry, as it were, before returning to a more humble and natural station in life.

Those familiar with some of the problems of organisation discussed in *The Art of Coarse Cricket* will probably note that the problems there have much in common with those raised by Coarse Bridge. The problems of Getting A Fixture, Getting A Team Together, Getting A Team To The Match, are fundamentally the same in both spheres. Getting the first fixture is in both cases nearly always an accident. You don't in Coarse Bridge, any more than you do in Coarse Cricket, decide—just like that—to arrange a game. If you receive an invitation to play from somebody in what may well have to be a pretty wide circle of friends (congenial card-table companions do not grow on trees), then your future is more or less assured. Before issuing their invitation your first hosts will have questioned you carefully to find out whether or not you qualify for the sort of bridge they play, in just the same way as you will have made certain what kind of bridge *they* play before you accept their invitation.

An invitation introduces you for the first time to at least two players (or three, if you are unaccompanied), who in turn are each likely to know a couple of other players, who in turn are each, etc., etc. In this way it is easy to build up a reserve of players and ensure continuity of fixtures.

To initiate the very first fixture yourself, on the other hand, is not easy. The subject of bridge can be raised casually during conversation in many kinds of company, and you can certainly learn in this way whether you are talking to bridge players or not. But considerable caution must be exercised in inviting people to come and play with you. When, on your mentioning the subject, they appear enthusiastic but qualify their enthusiasm with 'But I'm not very good, I'm afraid', take their name and number; their qualification is bound to be true (no Higher Bridge player would ever talk like that), and a drop of sincerity is worth a bucketful of earnestness and skill.

When you get the reply 'I used to play a lot, but I haven't played for ages now', put them down, too; the risk of earmarking a possible recruit who may not have played since Contract superseded Auction Bridge in 1929 is of no account. What is important is that he is clearly a nice chap who is happy to have played in his time and would enjoy the chance of playing again. He may have to be reminded of some of the conventions, or even the systems of scoring, that have become popular since he last played, but just as you never forget how to swim or ride a bicycle, so you never forget how to play bridge; and to explain a convention to somebody who has once played the game takes only a moment.

The type of player one should never consider asking to your card table (or taking to anyone else's) is one that the Coarse Bridge player will instinctively and immediately recognise. He is the sort of man who plays all his bridge at his club, not because he is a bachelor but because he doesn't consider his wife plays well enough. If by mischance you do not recognise him at once he will reveal himself in all his overpowering horror at the merest muttering of the word bridge. The fact that you were only talking about Waterloo Bridge to your neighbour in a pub is enough to bring the Bridge Bore (for that is who this man is) crashing into your conversation across any crowded room.

'Excuse me butting in, sir [there is never any escape from a stranger who calls you 'sir' or 'madam'], but I couldn't help hearing you talking about bridge. What a wonderful game, eh?' And with that you may bid farewell to tranquil mind, farewell content. You will hear a trick-by-trick account of the games he played last night, the night before, last Monday—no, not Monday, he had to take The Wife to the theatre; it must have been Tuesday. Yes, that's right, Tuesday; put 'em five down doubled and redoubled vulnerable, and then finished 'em off with a grand slam. If he hadn't led his Nine of Diamonds he'd have been in the soup, believe you him.

There are also Bridge Bores among women, but because they do not bore so loudly or so publicly they are not so often encountered as their male counterparts. They are, however, every bit as deadly as the male. The undesirable

Woman bridge bore

woman player will be as instinctively and immediately recognisable by the Coarse Bridge player as the undesirable man. It is not her conversation that gives her away, but a certain intenseness and ferocity of countenance, the deeply chiselled frown that can only have been made by the fury that Hell hasn't anything like when a woman's Significant Discard is scorned by her partner.

To such a woman bridge is no longer a game; it is a contest in which she strives to assert her superiority with all the aggressiveness which psychologists tell us men express by driving fast cars. She is a poor loser, and to be a few shillings down at the end of the evening is a misfortune she blames entirely on her partners, the cards she was dealt and the people who shuffled them.

Avoid her at all costs. Not that she'll want to know you, anyway, of course, which is quite a comfort.

As I have already suggested, the problem of Getting A Team Together to play bridge is not easily solved. Indeed, since the game to be played in fact involves only four people in the end, it is much more difficult to arrange successfully than a team for a Coarse Cricket match. To arrive two players short for cricket is not only standard practice but something of a miracle; you are usually at least four short, and your opponents help you out. But to be two players short for bridge can ruin everything and leave you and your wife playing gin rummy for the rest of the evening. Whereas in cricket your opponents help you out by making up the required numbers for you, in bridge a sudden shortage of players can result in a complete absence of opponents. The weather, too, can affect both games disastrously; the one because it is an outdoor game that cannot be played in the rain, the other because it is an indoor game that cannot be played if the hazards of floods, fog, snow and ice prevent players getting to—or, more often, from—the scene of the match.

These hazards are not so great in towns (though they can frighten all the taxis off the streets), but in the country they can often be serious, and we have spent many anxious winter hours waiting to hear that our guests have arrived home safely after setting out into a night of blizzards and six-foot snow-drifts that weren't there when play had begun earlier in the evening.

As with Coarse Cricket, the question of transport to and from the contest is an item that has to be carefully considered in the organisation of Coarse Bridge. In the years since the last war every government we've had has constantly interfered with the freedom of the British people to come and go as they please—not just abroad, but at home on the roads they mistakenly think their car licences pay for. If it wasn't petrol rationing because of the balance of payments it was petrol rationing because of Suez; and when petrol wasn't rationed they upped the tax on it once a year or more, and raised the road licence at the same time for good measure.

Petrol rationing (crossing our fingers) hasn't affected Coarse Bridge for some years now, but the institution of the annual Ministry of Transport test for cars has had irritating effects for those of us who live in the country. It is not that we have old crocks of cars; a car does not have to be more than three years old to be considered suspect by those incorrigible show-offs, the Ministers and Ministresses of Transport. In the country, where garages are few and labour is overworked, the process can leave you without any means of transport for a couple of days. Since the casual hailing of taxis or ordering of hire cars late at night is impossible, a game of bridge has to be so planned that the temporarily motor-less player is on somebody's route and can be given a lift.

The introduction of the breathalyser and blood-alcohol tests has so far not disturbed the strolling player of Coarse Bridge unduly. Like the only Metropolitan magistrate I know personally, most of my acquaintances regard the regulation as so ridiculous, and the 80 mg per pot per person maximum so unrealistic as a measure of intoxication, that the only thing to do is to observe it meticulously. In dealing with the people who dreamed up this law you are dealing with the mentally deficient, and it is wisest to humour them lest they grow violent and cause you bodily harm.

My friend the Metropolitan magistrate, incidentally, sighed wistfully for an English body with the independence and influence of the French Conseil National des Magistrats (or words to that effect), who answered with a resounding *Non!* when it was first proposed that French motorists should be subject to breathalyser or other alcohol tests. With unassailable logic, and as motorists and notorious trenchermen who were not entirely disinterested parties, MM les Magistrats de France asked what did the tests prove? Answer: the amount of alcohol in the blood. And what did that prove? Nothing.

There were some, the magistrates observed in the picturesque idiom of the country, who could get as drunk as a Pole, or a thrush, on a single *petit verre*; there were others who were as sober as a—well, as a magistrate, after a couple of litres. Case dismissed.

Where in Coarse Cricket the burden of Organisation seems to be borne only by the unfortunate captain who is trying to get a team together to go to the country for the day (your cricket opponents always live on the spot, of course, and have a long-established and efficient organisation of their own), in Coarse Bridge both sides are plagued with Organisation. The home side and the visiting team are likely to have the same difficulty in getting a team together and getting a team to the match; and though consultation between the two parties may bring temporary relief, nothing will alter the fact that the therapeutic effect of sharing one's troubles is nil—in the organisation of Coarse Bridge, at any rate.

3

Technique

CHOOSING PARTNERS

Choose what many men desire
SHAKESPEARE

ARRANGING who shall play with, or against, whom (which is very often the same thing) is traditionally decided by cutting the cards, thus at once introducing an element of reckless chance into the game before you have even sat down to play it. Whether those who cut the two highest cards, the two lowest, or the highest and the lowest should be paired together is a matter for mutual agreement.

Mutual agreement can also decide that partners can be allotted by arrangement without having to cut the cards at all. This can sometimes be a most profitable method, particularly if it enables you to choose a beginner as your partner. By a 'beginner' I don't mean people like you and me, who have been beginners for thirty years or more, but a genuine fledgeling of three or four months' eager experience who still has that priceless asset which the rest of us have lost long ago—beginner's luck.

A partner gifted with this will probably make hair-raising bids when silence would be golden, and remain obstinately tongue-tied and uncooperative when you have a sitting slam. Then, just when you have abandoned all hope, they restore your superstitious belief in the infallibility of beginner's luck by suddenly making an unintentionally brilliant defensive lead, or having a perfect dream of a hand which they bid like a master.

To *choose* a true beginner as a partner is a gamble, of course; their luck may not be active on the evening you are playing with them. But then we have never doubted that bridge was an out-and-out gambling game, and in consequence riddled with superstitions. If you cut the highest card in the ballot for partners—especially if it is an Ace—then you 'stay with it' and make everybody else move around, spilling their drinks, dropping their lighters and cigarettes and upsetting their ashtrays as they do so. If you have just won a rubber and your high card entitles you to deal as well as choose your seat, it is lucky to deal again with the pack that brought you victory.

It need hardly be emphasised that, if you are playing on your own home ground, old and well-thumbed cards should be used for as long as possible. They will bear many familiar marks of identification, such as stains, dog-ears and chipped edges, which, however hard you pretend to yourself that you are not taking advantage of them, cannot fail to enter into your subconscious and be of inestimable value in inspiring your 'psychic' certainty that the King of Spades—with its indelible red wine stains—is in the hand on your right. And if it is not—well, that's all in keeping with the sporting nature of bridge itself.

B

SHUFFLING AND DEALING

Patience, and shuffle the cards

CERVANTES

Shuffling, to the casual onlooker an innocent and uncomplicated operation, is in fact extremely difficult to perform well. Expert shuffling ensures a square deal for all; it is performed rapidly, thoroughly and with such neatness that the pack is tidied up and placed ready, and all but wrapped up in cellophane again, for the next hand long before the dealer has finished dealing.

This sort of shuffling is rarely found in Coarse Bridge, and indeed is not to be encouraged. The slow and fumbling, untidy redisposition of the cards in the pack which passes for shuffling with most of us may not be very efficient but it can lead to very interesting hands. The not-too-carefully-shuffled pack can be a considerable help in the course of play. At least one renowned international player advised his readers, when executing a tricky finesse of a Queen, to play on the assumption that the Queen lay over the Jack; he argued that the cards were likely to have been imperfectly shuffled after the previous deal and that it was worth gambling on the Queen having covered the Jack on that occasion.

As for methods of shuffling, the most impressive is to divide the pack into two parts, place them close to each other on the table and interlock the cards from each pile with your thumbs, making a noise like a machine gun as you do it. The most important and imposing feature of this method is the noise. You may repeat the process several times without in fact once allowing the two stacks of cards to come into contact with each other at all (let alone intermingle), and nobody will doubt that you are

Shuffling and dealing

shuffling with great dexterity. It is the noise that convinces those who hear it of the professional competence of your performance.

That the standard of shuffling is generally rather low— or, shall we say, not altogether thorough—is suggested not only by the expert and his Queen finesse quoted above but by no less a figure than Ely Culbertson himself: he warns you that if there is a singleton or a blank suit in one hand there will nearly always be a compensatory singleton or blank suit in another. Or perhaps that hasn't anything to do with shuffling but is just another gambler's superstition.

The other method of shuffling, which is executed by holding half the cards in the palm of the hand and trying to mix the other half into them, takes a long time—mainly because the process is interrupted by cards continually dropping on the floor and having to be picked up again. The delay caused by this has considerable psychological effect, and as shuffler you may deduce a great deal from the impatience or dejection shown by the other three players who have already arranged and studied their cards long before you have got round to picking yours up. The poker face is not encountered often in Coarse Bridge.

The purpose of shuffling the pack is, of course, to redistribute the cards. But there is redistribution and redistribution. On certain occasions you may recognise in the hand you are dealt the exact cards you remember dummy having had the last time the pack was used. You should be able to work out from this which of the other three players has got your hand this time—that is, if you can remember what cards you had that long while ago, which is unlikely.

These freakish strokes of fortune, however, are merely

sent to try you and are very rarely of any use to anybody except your opponents, who will take one look at dummy and at once work out where every card lies.

You will note that, regardless of the eccentric hands which can crop up from time to time in Coarse Bridge, there is no question of re-shuffling. 'Re-shuffling' is a term invented by politicians to give the impression that astonishingly forward-looking, if not actually pragmatic, changes are being made in the Cabinet. It is obvious that their knowledge of cards—except the Three-Card Trick—is as shaky as their knowledge of the meaning of the word shuffle; if Prime Ministers played Coarse Bridge they would know that 're-shuffling' a pack of Ministers, whom we must suppose to have already been shuffled, would do nothing but change the order of the collection of Yarboroughs they dealt out in the first place. It is an unfortunate metaphor, and even though one knows what they think they mean by promising a New Deal, what the politicians ought to do is give up beggar-my-neighbour and try another game altogether—like bridge, for instance, where they have to make what they contract to do, or go down and pay heavily for it.

The bridge pack, having been shuffled and cut, eventually finds its way to the dealer, who, if he is dealing at your table for the first time, has to be watched rather carefully. It is the tradition in bridge to deal out one card at a time, starting with the player on the dealer's left. There are times, however, when a poker or pontoon player obliges by making a fourth for you and will deal the cards two at a time to each player. If you feel terribly strongly about this departure from convention you should, naturally, ask the dealer to start again, one at a time, and not to ask if the recipient wants it 'twisted' or not.

If you don't mind, of course, it really makes absolutely no difference to the sort of hand you get whether you are given your cards two at a time or all thirteen in one individual lot at once. The chances of being dealt a good or bad hand by these or any other irregular methods are neither better nor worse than those offered by the traditional dealing of a bridge hand. But at least they relieve the monotony of the one-for-you, one-for-him, one-for-her, one-for-me routine.

CONVENTIONS

> There is none that doeth good, no not one. . . . They are altogether become abominable
>
> PSALM XIV

As soon as the cards have been shuffled, cut, misdealt and placed in position for re-dealing, the final deal need only be delayed until the dealer returns from the kitchen where she has had to run quickly to turn down the oven and her husband has finished looking helplessly for tonic water in the dresser instead of the fridge; it should then be only a matter of moments before the session can begin. That is, if you have remembered to discuss conventions with your partner. Even if you have played with them before—say as recently as last evening—it is still a wise move to discuss conventions, as they may well have adopted a new one in the interval.

This assumes that your partner plays a convention at all. There are still players to be found who, having started life with Auction Bridge, have stayed with it. I once spent a weekend in the country where one of my fellow house-guests announced quite bluntly as he sat down at the bridge table for the first rubber that he just did not

believe in conventions. Like the author of the Thirty-
Nine Articles, he regarded them as blasphemous fables
and dangerous deceits.

'Why should I tell everybody what I've got in my
hand?' he asked indignantly.

We repeated the standard definition of a convention
as an arrangement between partners whereby a bid or
play has a particular, possibly artificial, meaning.

'That's all very well,' the Flat Earth enthusiast persisted, 'but I still don't see why I should tell my opponents
what I've got in my hand and they're bound to hear.'

One must admit he had a point there. A lot of bidding
seems designed to tell your opponents everything and
your partner nothing.

Once you have decided to adopt a convention the
question arises: which one? Personal preference may be
for the Two Club, but with the modern proliferation of
systems, due to the extension of mass communication
and all that, you may well find yourself with a partner
who doesn't know the Two Club convention from a bull's
foot, but is addicted to another which—they think—is
called the Abol, or the Cuthbertson, or the Lockstock
and Blackwell.

Inevitably this involves a great deal of discussion
between you and your partner (to say nothing of the
discussion that is going on between your opponents, who
are having the same trouble). Your final persuasion of
your partner that the Two Club convention is likely to
suit your common purpose better than any other (especially as it is the only one you personally happen to know)
is usually a matter of perseverance if they don't know the
convention; what better time to adopt it than this very
moment? You will explain the finer points as you go
along—if you get the cards for it, that is.

Coarse Bridge being the kind of game it mercifully is, one is always permitted, and indeed, well advised, to interrupt the flow of the bidding by asking openly (begging your opponents' leave) what you ought to say after your partner's Two Club opening when you want to show that you have nine Diamonds to the Ten, a singleton Heart, the Three and Four of Clubs, and no Spades. The Two Club system, you will be told, has the exact answer for this: there has been a misdeal. A re-count of your hand shows that it in fact contains three small Hearts; two of them got mixed up with the red Diamonds, which are now shown to consist of eight to the Ten—making the regulation thirteen cards in all. The Two Club system can find a call to fit this hand too, though what it is escapes me for the moment.

The opening bid of Two Clubs, intended to show that you have at least 5 H.T. (H.T. means Honour Tricks in Bridge, as it means Hybrid Tea in gardening and High Tension in electricity), inevitably—unless your partner answers negatively from the start—involves you in the Blackwood 4–5 No Trump convention. The purpose of this is to learn from your partner first how many Aces and then how many Kings he holds, with a view to looking for a slam. Why at this stage in the bidding it should be necessary to embark on an elaborate code which deceives nobody, not even your partner, isn't quite clear. Instead of bidding Four No Trumps to find out from your partner's reply of Five Diamonds that he has one Ace, surely it would be much simpler to ask your partner in so many words 'How many Aces, partner?' then how many Kings, and when he's told you none, one, two or whatever, you can decide whether you want to bid a small slam or a grand slam or not.

Apart from anything else, *is* the Blackwood Convention as crystal clear as its adherents maintain it is? According to one of the famous bridge pedagogues, 'With no Aces (also four Aces) partner will respond Five Clubs. . . .' There's ambiguity for you. If you ask for Aces and your partner's response can mean he has four, where did he get them from? You've already got two in your own hand, otherwise you couldn't have opened Two Clubs in the first place. But perhaps partner is using a different pack, or keeps the odd H.T. up his sleeve. And if you haven't any Aces yourself, what did you bid Two Clubs on? Four pairs of Kings and Queens, which add up to only 4 H.T.?

On the other hand, to simplify bidding to the extent of asking a straight question for a straight answer could take a lot of fun out of the game and would deny your opponents the luxury of being able to interrupt from time to time with an unexpected Double or a wild call of Seven Diamonds, which might push you into a grand slam you can't make, or into a double that will still make it cheaper for your unvulnerable opponents to go down, than for you to make your Six Hearts.

To be honest, the Two Club system itself is bewildering enough already to many people, without having to drag in Blackwood—which was obviously invented by the late Algernon Blackwood as part of his life-work of inventing tales of the Uncanny and the Supernatural. It is a common occurrence for your opening Two Club bid to be misunderstood by your partner as well as your opponents, for in spite of the general and detailed discussion of the positive and negative conventional responses which follows all Two Club openings in Coarse Bridge, your partner's eventual denial of Two Diamonds is sure to be followed by one of your opponents asking the question: 'Does that mean two *real* Diamonds?' And the whole system has to be explained again.

Actually, nobody at the table with an eye or an ear has any need to wait for the actual oral statement of a strong-two bid in any convention. Not only will one look at the facial expression of anybody picking up a 5 H.T. hand tell you at once, but they will interrupt the normal conversation that is still going on about the last hand after the next has been dealt with impatient enquiries about whose bid it is. 'Did I deal this? No, it must have been Annabelle.' As I said: a poker face is an unfamiliar sight at the Coarse Bridge table.

The only Coarse Bridge player with a poker face I ever knew of was one who was frequently forced by family circumstances to make up a very reluctant and inexpert fourth at an otherwise high-class table (his wife was an exceptionally brilliant player). Archie was an eminent ear, nose and throat surgeon and when asked what kind of bridge he played, answered firmly, 'British Bridge!'— no conventions or any damn Yankee nonsense like that. When the other players insisted that he must surely observe a convention of *some* kind, Archie would admit well, yes, he did: the Hickey-Peart convention.

The puzzled response to this deadpan announcement was met by Archie with incredulous surprise. Everybody knew the Hickey-Peart convention; it was really too elementary to need explaining. The odd thing was that such a convention apparently did exist. Archie had read about it in an article in Scotland many years before, and had adopted it as a defence against exploitation by his superiors. The only trouble was that he had forgotten what it actually consisted of, otherwise there is no doubt that he would have explained it to his partner and insisted on playing it. As it was, he just played it anyway and found that it functioned very well—as far as he was concerned. (Incidentally, the Two Club system is sometimes referred to as 'British style', so perhaps Archie with his 'British Bridge' got nearer to playing a familiar convention than he knew.)

Obviously, if it can be done by the Culbertsons and Gorens and Fishbeins and the group of gentlemen from Hampstead who played in Acol Road, N.W. 6, and named a system after it, anybody can be allowed to evolve a convention; and, if you ask me, a lot of people have. For instance, there is one where instead of responding to a Four No Trump search for Aces by bidding Five Clubs if you have either no Aces or the complete set, you bid Four Clubs to ask for Aces and Five Diamonds shows all or nothing.

There is another known as the One Club system where, of all things, if you have a strong hand you open One Club (weakness response: One Diamond). If you want to open a normal One Club you say Two Clubs, and if you open Two Hearts or Two Spades this means that you're all right but not strong enough to open One Club.

This last system seems to bear some resemblance to what is called the Indian Club convention, where an opening bid of One Club shows five Quick Tricks, at least three of which must be in the red suits. The positive response to this, which also shows Aces (why not show them at once, after all, instead of hanging about?), is One No Trump (one Ace or four Aces) or Two Clubs for two Aces. If you have more than two Aces the response is Three Clubs, which asks your partner what the hell he opened on unless he was blank in the two black suits. If he was, then he must show the stronger of the two red suits in his hand by calling Four Clubs to show Diamonds (which will promptly be doubled by the other side, who are strong in Clubs and don't know why it is sometimes called the Red Indian Club system); or Five Clubs to show Hearts (which will also promptly be doubled by the opposition, who are strong in Spades and don't know why, etc.).

From this point on, the progress towards bidding a slam is easy. The original caller bids Six Clubs, his partner responds Six Diamonds, and if that doesn't suit his hand, the original caller bids Six Hearts. There can never be a slam in the Red Indian Club convention except in Diamonds or Hearts. If you want a slam in Clubs, Spades or No Trumps you have to use the ordinary Two Club opening.

The negative response to the Red Indian Club opening is One Diamond (no Aces), which enables the opener, if he is now in trouble, to sign off leaving it in One Diamond if that is the stronger of his two red suits or switching to One Heart if it isn't. His partner will know to pass.

The denial response of One Diamond confuses the opposition nine times out of ten, even though you will, of course, have explained the principles of the convention to the assembled company before the game began. As can be seen, I think, from this brief description the Red Indian Club system has many useful features, among them its air of guileless simplicity which can deceive your opponents, the early stage in the bidding at which Aces can be shown and, above all, the impossibility of reaching a game call on Indian Club bidding. It is a red suit slam or nothing. Usually nothing.

If you want to play the hand in Clubs in the normal way you just announce that you are going to open One

Ordinary Club—a move clearly permitted by the definition of a convention (laid down I forget where) which states that it is 'Any call or play which, by agreement or understanding between partners, serves to convey a meaning other than would be attributed to it by the opponents in the absence of an explanation.' If you announce to your partner and your opponents that you are calling One Ordinary Club there is no possible chance of being accused of ambiguity. You have explained everything, as asked.

If the objection is raised that it is not done to change conventions in mid-rubber, let alone in mid-hand, you can meet it by suggesting it is time it was. Provided he warns the batsman a right-handed bowler can change to bowling left-handed in a cricket match; the same freedom to change tactics should be regarded as permissible in a democratic game like bridge.

It may make all the difference between winning and losing, and who wants to lose—even in Coarse Bridge?

BIDDING

> All the perfumes of Arabia will not sweeten this little hand
>
> SHAKESPEARE

When it comes to bidding it is everybody's first hope that they will be able to make not a wild call, but what the late Poet Laureate went on to describe as a clear call that may not be denied. That is everybody's hope.

In practice, however, it is not so much what you've got in your hand and want to call, as what your partner has and doesn't, or hasn't but will all the same.

There are three stages in the career of all who play

Coarse Bridge. The first is when you pray that your hand is so poor that you will not have to bid at all in case you have to play it. The second stage is the feeling of panic when you have responded to your partner's opening suit bid with a non-committal One No Trump to keep it open, and you find that unless you can introduce another suit— *any* suit—you will have to play the hand in No Trumps. The third stage is when you want to play the hand in *your* suit and go on bidding it however hard your partner tries to talk you out of it.

These attitudes, it will be noticed, are all defensive, and characteristic of that insecurity which any Freudian will tell you leads inevitably to aggressiveness. And one quickly learns that it is only a step from the timid silence of the first stage to the forceful obstinacy of the third. There is not much the more experienced and less mixed-up player can do about these unpredictable fledgeling partners, except pick them up when they fall out of the nest, dust them off, and hope they'll learn to fly soon. The only trouble is that it is debatable whether their eventual self-confidence is better than their early lack of it.

Conventions are intended to cover most of the contingencies encountered in bidding, but there are still a number of bids needed for what one might call supra-conventional purposes—bids that will help the caller out of a dilemma which his cards, not his partner or the convention, have placed him in at a given moment in the auction.

There is no bid more urgently needed, for instance, than that of the simple opening bid consisting of the one word 'Double'. It is pure pedantry to suggest that you've got to have something to double, and as this is an opening bid nobody has so far made any bid that can be doubled.

Time and again one has picked up a hand which contains the sort of distribution and strength that is a perfect hand to double anything—bid or unbid.

True, if this method is to be logically applied, an opening bid of Double by South must be liable to a re-double by West. If North and East both passed then South would have to try a suit, knowing already from West's re-double that *that* is where the opposition's strength lies. If West passes, of course, then North must make some sort of response to South's opening Double— calling One Club to keep the bidding low.

What should happen after that is anybody's guess, for the Strong Double convention has not yet been developed beyond the opening and answering bids, but it is obvious that something along these lines is needed.

The experts, of course, recognise this need—none better—and are constantly devising new forms of bidding which can be introduced to extend the vocabulary of the conventions without actually passing their hands across the table for their partners to look at.

The use of the so-called 'Herbert' negative, for instance, is intended as an advance in communication that bridges the gulf between partners across the table. (Perhaps that use of the word 'bridges' is a clue to the origin of the game's name. It is as good a solution as many I've seen put forward.) In practice it can prove a little ambiguous. Whoever 'Herbert' may have been, his method apparently offers solace to those who, having opened a Strong Two, prefer an alternative to the traditional denial of Two No Trumps.

'Herbert's' negative is three of the next higher-ranking suit. But if the opening is Two Spades, is the next higher-ranking suit Three Clubs, or Two No Trumps, which is, after all, a higher bid than Two Spades? It is the sort of confusion which, when it involves the class of players the bridge columnists write about, brings considerable joy to the heart of the Coarse Bridge players.

A typical 'Herbert' situation was reported recently in which South opened Two Spades and North denied with Three Clubs, believing, quite logically, that Clubs were the higher-ranking *suit* since Two No Trumps cannot be. South, for his part, regarded Two No Trumps as the immediately superior bid to Two Spades and interpreted North's Three Clubs as a positive and genuine jump call.

West interpreted it that way too, and so did East, who had a handful of Clubs to the Ace, King, Ten and naturally doubled—a bid which (since North's Clubs were supposed to be genuine) West imagined could only be a take-out to one of the unbid suits. He accordingly led the Ace of Diamonds, which was a blank suit in South's hand, and a small slam was made in Spades that shouldn't have been.

The hands looked like this:

```
                    S: 8 6 2
                    H: 10 6 3
                    D: K 10 6 5 2
                    C: Q 8

    S: Q 10       ┌──────────┐      S: 5 4
    H: J 4 2      │     N    │      H: K
    D: A Q 9 3    │  W     E │      D: J 8 7 4
    C: 9 7 6 5    │     S    │      C: A K 10 4 3 2
                  └──────────┘

                    S: A K J 9 7 3
                    H: A Q 9 8 7 5
                    D: ──────
                    C: J
```

The bidding went South: Two Spades—West: No bid
—North: Three Clubs—East: Double—South: Three
Hearts—West: No bid—North: Four Spades—East: No
bid—South: Six Spades.

Obviously 'Herbert', applied to an opening Two
Spades, does what no other negative bid can do—
successfully confuse your partner, both your opponents
and yourself, all at the same time.

They were a pretty muddled couple anyway, that North
and South. Having decided to play 'Herbert', which
excludes the traditional Two No Trumps denial of an
opening Strong Two, why should North ever have
imagined it could be the next higher-ranking suit, which
is what the negative response demands?

Bridge championship internationals, it is reassuring to
know, can get their heads so full of fancy artificial bids
that the auction begins to sound like a bazaar, with East
and West wanting to know what on earth North and
South are talking about, which is by no means clear to
North and South themselves.

Terence Reese tells of a dialogue at Oslo which ran
something like this:

North (*who was a Mr Flint and playing the Flint-Pender
convention which 'contains a number of artificial bids over Two
No Trumps'*): Two No Trumps.

East: Pass.

South (*who was Mr Reese and 'chanced to recall' that Four
Diamonds would signify a minor two-suit hand*): Four
Diamonds.

West: Pass.

North: Four Spades.

East: What did Four Diamonds mean?

North (*hesitantly*): I assume it was Texas, asking me to
transfer to Four Spades.

Nobody had mentioned Texas; North merely 'assumed' South was using it. It was a pity East had to ask his question about Four Diamonds; North and South might otherwise have got themselves in a pretty pickle that would have been well worth seeing.

In Coarse Bridge, of course, the mere act of bidding gets all the players into a pickle and everybody asks questions all the time; they have to, otherwise the hand would never get played. Even in Coarse Bridge, where, regardless of the nature of the hands dealt, discussion and bidding and questions are general and free-for-all, there are nevertheless very often moments when one pair of partners will find it more fun to keep quiet and heed the Fool's advice to King Lear:

> Have more than thou showest,
> Speak less than thou knowest . . .

This is when they are playing against a couple who play the Hammer-and-Tongs system. These players, usually husband and wife, are quite violent in their determination that the hand shall be played in the suit *they* bid. Interspersed between the monotonous No Bids from the opposition, the bids grow in ferocity and extravagance in a relentless sequence.

'One Club.'
'One Diamond.'
'Two Clubs.'
'Two Diamonds.'
'Three Clubs.'
'Three Diamonds.'
'Five Clubs'.

This is intended as a shut-out game call, but is ignored by partner who retaliates with Five Diamonds, another

Hammer-and-Tongs system

shut-out game call. This drives the opener still higher to
Six Clubs.

'Six Diamonds,' answers partner.

'Seven Clubs.'

'Seven Diamonds.'

At this point the opposition, coming out of the hypnotic
fascination exercised by their opponents over-calling each
other remorselessly—as though, instead of being partners,
each was fighting to prevent the other scoring vital game,
rubber, and world championship match points—at this
point the opposition doubles.

North, deprived of his Seven Clubs slam, decides to
teach his partner a lesson and redoubles.

The following hands are then played:

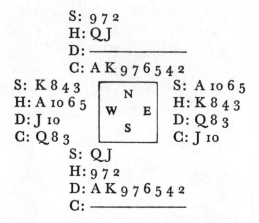

```
              S: 9 7 2
              H: Q J
              D: ──────────
              C: A K 9 7 6 5 4 2
S: K 8 4 3    ┌──────────┐   S: A 10 6 5
H: A 10 6 5   │    N     │   H: K 8 4 3
D: J 10       │ W      E │   D: Q 8 3
C: Q 8 3      │    S     │   C: J 10
              └──────────┘
              S: Q J
              H: 9 7 2
              D: A K 9 7 6 5 4 2
              C: ──────────
```

West leads his Ace of Hearts, dummy goes down on
the table and the Thurber-like Battle of the Sexes is
fought in silence by North and South, reaching its climax
at Trick 13 when the irreconcilable North-South partner-
ship goes 6 down (vulnerable, of course), doubled and

redoubled, to the tune of 3400 points. And not even a
hundred for honours.

The post mortem is acrimonious, to say the least. Why,
asks North, didn't South shut up when he called Five
Clubs, which was a game call? Because, retorts South, it
was obvious to anybody but a selfish halfwit like North
that the hand had to be played in Diamonds. It is then
pointed out by the opposition that even if North or South
had left the bidding at Five Clubs or Five Diamonds they
would still have gone four down.

For the rest of the rubber the Hammer-and-Tongs
family sulk; they pass everything, in spite of having quite
good cards, and allow their opponents to progress slowly
and comfortably, by a series of part scores, to win the
rubber with One Spade, One No Trump and One
Heart.

If the word 'psychic' means anything at all, it ought to
be applied to the sort of bidding discussed above, inas-
much as it was clearly influenced, according to the
dictionary, by 'phenomena and conditions apparently
outside the domain of physical law'. The auction also
demonstrated the meaning of the 'pre-emptive' bid in its
most effective form, which not only shut out opponents
at a very high level, but created an atmosphere that made
it difficult for them to enter the bidding at the opening
level of One Club.

It is obvious from this that bridge terms can mean
different things to different people. I have seen the
phrase 'psychic' bid defined in one text book as a 'bluff'
bid. What is not quite clear from this is who is supposed
to be bluffing whom—whether the caller is bluffing his
partner or his opponents, or both.

To most of us the commonest 'psychic' bid is the No

Psychic bids

Bid in response to a partner who, after much dithering
and counting with his fingers (from the number of times
he's tapped on the table it is difficult to tell if he has
arrived at a point count of 40 or 6, or is just fidgeting),
has opened an unconvincing One Diamond. This 'psychic'
bid is also known as the Strong No, and is based on the
telepathic certainty that the opener is over-valuing his
hand with One Diamond and that any encouragement
would end in double, double, toil and trouble.

The Weak No, another 'psychic' bid delivered in a
noticeably different, preferably hopeless, tone of voice, is
intended not only to discourage your partner when
he has opened or over-called, but also to deceive your
opponents into believing that a number of vital cards they
want to know about (as you intend that they shall play
the hand) must be in your partner's hand, whereas they
are in fact in yours.

The so-called 'asking' bid, though rarely used nowadays
in the early stages of the bidding in other classes of
bridge, is of course still an indispensable and familiar
feature of Coarse Bridge. It differs, however, from what
was generally considered an 'asking' bid, in the elasticity
and the colour of the language in which the questions
are asked and answered. The most common asking bid
runs something like this:

'Excuse me asking, but if June doubles, what do I say
if I want to tell Geoffrey I've got the Ace of his suit but
otherwise it's a Yarborough? Should I leave him in One
Heart?'

The 'cue' bid is seldom made in Coarse Bridge, but when
it is—by a player who has stayed awake reading a
Sunday newspaper bridge article and wants to try it out

and see what happens—it is a cue for a flood of questions from all sides. And not surprisingly, for what on earth can East be talking about when he calls Two Diamonds over North's One Diamond over-call of West's opening One Club?

East has to explain that his is a 'cue' bid; all right, but a cue for what? Hardly for a song and dance by West, who is completely perplexed until he learns that East's call means that he has control of Diamonds. West doesn't think much of this; why didn't East double like anybody else?

'Well, you see,' says East—but he says no more; his lips are sealed. He looks very smug about it.

South, whose partner had called Diamonds, hesitates for a moment, undecided whether to double or join in the imperfectly understood 'cue'-bid game and bid Three Clubs to show that he has a guard in West's opening suit. He decides on Three Clubs.

West doubles, which is a cue for East, when North bids Three Diamonds, to call Five Clubs. All pass. As it happens West makes Seven Clubs on his ear, but like his two opponents he doesn't realise until he sees dummy that what East had been trying to tell him was that he had no Diamonds at all.

There is naturally some resentful discussion of this by North, South and West (particularly West), but East insists firmly that a 'cue' bid is a 'cue' bid, and if he wants to show control of Diamonds by having a void naturally he has to bid Diamonds.

The practice of bidding a suit you haven't got is not to be encouraged in Coarse Bridge. It is difficult enough to know how to bid the suit you *have* got without embarking on paradoxes that drag the game down to the level of international economics and all its chicanery, and East is forcefully advised to give up reading bridge articles which only give him ideas above his station.

In the study of bidding so far in this chapter no detailed mention has been made of the 'pre-emptive' bid. That is because in Coarse Bridge the 'pre-emptive', or 'shut-out', bid doesn't mean quite what it does elsewhere. Too often a confident opening bid of Three Hearts will not only fail to silence the opposition, but will incite them to call Four Spades, thus smartly shutting out the original pre-empter and his partner. The state of the score naturally affects these 'pre-emptive' bids, and in Coarse Bridge it is wise to have a look at everybody else's score-card as well as your own, and even that is not altogether reliable.

There is likely to be a considerable discrepancy between the scores recorded by your left- and your right-hand neighbours, and it is something of a coincidence if your score tallies with your partner's. A general check of score-cards usually puts things right, but not for long. Scores that belong above the line are included below it, part-scores are put above the line and your opponents seem to enjoy 50 per cent bonus of some kind that makes their Club and Diamond tricks worth 30 points as against the 20 you get for yours. And the price of ensuring that your opponents do not credit themselves with 40 points for every trick in No Trumps is a ceaseless vigilance, and the sort of surreptitious overlooking of what your neighbours are writing down that is normally found only in examination rooms.

It is characteristic of the liberal spirit that distinguishes Coarse Bridge that the question of suit preference in bidding should be elastic and liable to highly individual interpretation. True, there are some players who treat the matter with solemn mathematical concern, balancing the point-count of one suit against another and that sort of thing; but personal aesthetic and superstitious feelings are what really affect the player's choice of a suit he wishes to back.

Some like the two major suits, on the principle that not so many tricks are needed for game. Others, with a soft spot for the underdog, favour the minor suits. That suits are chosen for the qualities found in them by William Cowper is certainly possible. He spoke in his poem 'The Task' of

> . . . spots quadrangular of di'mond form,
> Ensanguin'd hearts, clubs typical of strife,
> And spades, the emblem of untimely graves.

(Cowper, incidentally, obviously knew and enjoyed his Coarse Bridge; it was in the same poem that he first wrote: 'Variety's the very spice of life, That gives it all its flavour.')

But, mainly, since cards are instruments of chance, the Coarse Bridge player takes a gypsy-like view of the suits, preferring Diamonds because they're for ever, Clubs because they are symbols of virility or aggressiveness, Hearts because the bidder's in love, Spades because they are sinister and symbols of Death (remember Carmen).

A quartet of players familiar with each other's personalities and psychology will, of course, be able to read each other's hands like a book in these circumstances, and by simple deduction know that anything their partners or opponents may bid ain't necessarily so. This, in short, is real 'psychic' bidding, with partner and opponents, not the caller, having to have a sixth sense in interpreting the phenomena it throws up.

In the course of its evolution Contract Bridge has naturally altered or entirely discarded many of the rules that regulated the play of Auction Bridge. Some of these rules, I feel, might well be looked at and introduced into Coarse Bridge to the game's advantage.

For instance, there could be no rule whose adoption would be more welcome than the one which in Auction Bridge lays down that 'should a player bid out of turn the player on his left may demand a new deal'. It would require no great skill or subtlety to induce an opponent to speak out of turn, especially when it is clear from his facial expression that he is dying to call; which is why, of course, you would like to get rid of your own rotten cards —what Macbeth called 'thy bloody and invisible hand', and Hamlet 'the hand of little employment'—and get a new lot.

Having freed itself from the rule in Auction Bridge that dummy may not warn declarer against leading from the wrong hand, Contract Bridge could surely afford to accept the penalty (or reward) of a new deal for an out-of-turn bid.

Exactly how easy it is to encourage careless talk (getting an out-of-turn bid is child's play) can be gathered from the classic situation which developed in a recent international Coarse Bridge tournament. In the midst of lively general conversation South cunningly pretended he had not put down the score of the previous game and quietly asked West what they had made.

West replied: 'Two Clubs.'

South (*writing it down*): Oh yes. That makes it 80 below.

North (*having heard West say Two Clubs*): No bid.

East (*who has also heard West say Two Clubs, gives a negative response*): Two Diamonds.

South: No bid.

West, believing that East's Two Diamonds is a Strong Two opening, and having six Diamonds to the nine, jumps to Five Diamonds, a game call and a score they don't need as they already have 80 towards game.

North passes. East passes. South doubles.

West and East, who are vulnerable, realise they have been tricked when dummy goes down. West is furious and asks how the hell East dare open a Strong Two with one and a half quick tricks and a blank in Diamonds.

'I wasn't opening a Strong Two; it was a denial of Two Clubs.'

'Who said anything about Two Clubs?'

'You did.'

'I certainly didn't!'

North intervenes and remarks quietly to West: 'You did, you know. That's why I said No Bid.' And turning to South: 'Didn't he?'

South agrees.

West protests that he couldn't possibly have opened Two Clubs with a hand like his. Nothing like five quick tricks in it.

South looks innocent: 'I must say I thought you were being a little optimistic.'

After some philosophical shrugging of shoulders all round, and muttering about bridge being only a game after all, the hand is played and North and South put declarer and his partner down nine tricks, doubled and vulnerable, to the tune of 2600 points.

Why didn't North and South enter the bidding? Because having played this cunning convention for years (it can only be used when the opposition have reached a part score of 80 with Two Clubs in the previous hand), they know even if they can make an unvulnerable small slam themselves it can only bring them 690 points at best, whereas by using the Careless Talk convention they can net another 1910 points and have a lot of fun as well.

Of course, there is always a possibility that West's involuntary Two Clubs might in effect prove genuine, or that East might have a positive response to the imagined Two Club opening. In that case there might still be some interesting and unusual bridge.

In addition to the familiar 'psychic', 'pre-emptive' and 'cue' bids already discussed, there are signs of a growing use in Coarse Bridge of what is known as the 'protective' bid. This should not be encouraged. Some of us may consider that we have successfully used this convention for years—as a means of protecting partner against himself, when he has bid up to three in a minor suit and you sense that unless you pass emphatically (the 'protective' bid is negative as well as positive) the idiot will find himself trying to play a game contract of Five.

In its more usual form the protective bid is designed to help a partner who has refrained from bidding because he doesn't want to show what he's got in his hand at that stage, rather than to restrain a partner who will not stop bidding because he wants to show it at all costs. The protective bid is made fourth in hand after South, the dealer, has bid one of a suit, your partner West has passed, and North has passed.

For some reason you (East) think your partner may have made what is called a 'trap pass', though whom he is aiming to trap, and into what, is not quite clear. Anyway, instead of letting your opponents stew in One Club and good luck to them, you are psychic and shrewd enough to guess that your partner has more in his hand than has so far met the ear. Your hand is

S: K J 10 5
H: K 5 3
D: Q 10 8 3
C: 4 2

—so you 'protect' your partner's pass by bidding One Spade. His 'trap' may have been not to tell anybody that his best suit was Clubs and that he had South's opening One Club covered; or it may not. The purpose of 'protecting' his pass is to cheer him up and perhaps pick up a part score.

Of course, if West has genuinely passed because he has nothing, then whatever trap there is seems to fool nobody but East, who may well be left to protect himself and his interests in one miserable, perhaps unattainable, Spade.

The objections to accepting the protective bid as a feature of Coarse Bridge are fairly obvious from this example. What player of the game would know what a 'trap pass' was, let alone how to make it or ensure that his partner would recognise it if he heard it? And the idea that any player with a hand he could eventually bid might ever wait for his partner to provide him with a 'protective' bid before speaking is so out of character as to be beyond comment. There is a limit to artificiality, even—or particularly—in Coarse Bridge.

'Preventive' bidding, on the other hand, is another matter; it is familiar to all players of Coarse Bridge and is the nearest the game ever gets to what the experts mean by the 'pre-emptive' bid. The difference is that the 'preventive' bid is not intended to shut out your opponents so much as your partner. The state of the score-card is immaterial; you open, and hope to close, the bidding with the Preventive Four of a minor suit, or Preventive Three of a major suit. These calls may incidentally bring you game, but their object is to allow you to play a hand quietly in the suit you fancy, which in your judgment will not lead to your being doubled or going too many down. As you only bid on a hand with three quick tricks in it you shouldn't do too badly.

The 'preventive' bid is not to be confused with the 'prohibitive' bid. This is another ironical name for the Hammer-and-Tongs system discussed on page 46 and is completely ineffective. It is a mere courtesy title.

Finally, there is the Romeo-and-Juliet, or Parting-is-such-sweet-sorrow, bid. This is practised late at night by a player who, instead of throwing his hand in like the rest of the company and hoping a new deal will settle the final rubber at last, keeps bidding a solitary One, which is passed *nem. con.* The bid never achieves so much as a part score because the declarer invariably goes one down or more, and will continue to do so until his partner and opponents between them raise enough tricks to inflict the *coup de grâce* on the unconscionably protracted evening.

The Romeo-and-Juliet bidder is fortunately not very common in Coarse Bridge circles, and when he appears he is found to be very much younger than his table companions, who are old and grey and beginning to be full of sleep around midnight. With any luck it soon becomes obvious to him that his enthusiasm and methods are not generally welcome and that his opponents would willingly let him make a spectacular slam as finale to the evening's play rather than go on saying One of something until it be morrow or later.

PLAYING THE HAND

> When in doubt, win the trick
> HOYLE (1672–1769)

There is no moment in life quite like that when dummy puts down the hand he thinks he has been telling you about and which you now have to play. It can be a moment of tragedy, of comedy, of tears, of laughter, when your worst fears are confirmed or your highest hopes surpassed, when anxiety and apprehension grip you or your spirits soar, when you wish you had bid more or regret you didn't bid less, when you wish you had been more courageous or are sorry you ever opened your mouth at all. It is a moment of the greatest elation, or the deepest, blackest despair.

The moment of laying his cards on the table is also an important one for dummy himself and it provides him with a variety of opportunities for dramatic display and expression.

The tempo at which he lays down his cards and the order in which he does so can create an effect of highly theatrical suspense. The Exposure Triumphant, if properly executed, can be a spectacular *tour de force*, a manifestation of pride in holding—if not actually having created personally—a hand which is laid on the table with great pomp and deliberation, building up card-by-card from the weakest suit (which includes Ace and Ten) in a crescendo of honour tricks and including, as a confidently timed climax, the revelation of a blank suit.

With any luck dummy will earn from the declarer a heart-felt 'Thank you, partner'. To address anybody as 'partner' in Coarse Bridge is a sure sign that you are content with what they have. Christian names, in my experience, are used between players only in moments of recrimination or horror; and if you hear married partners address each other as 'darling' then you know there's going to be trouble.

The Exposure Defiant is one of the most common of dummy's performances. This consists of laying down an extremely mediocre hand very quickly and in silence, except for a snort that unmistakably means 'I told you so, but you would go on bidding'.

The Exposure Optimistic is a very modest hand indeed, laid down without fuss while dummy explains his support of his partner's bidding with 'I knew you were bound to have something'.

The Exposure Obstinate is also a very modest hand, but laid down this time in a rather surly manner and accompanied by dummy's quite unjustifiable praise both of its quality and his bidding of it. Declarer tells him he should have left it in One Heart, instead of jumping to Four Hearts.

'What's the good of One Heart?' retorts dummy.

'It would have given us game,' explains declarer.

'Well, so does Four Hearts.'

Finally, there is the Exposure Penitent, a miserably undistinguished hand which dummy lays down with apologies sympathetically declined by declarer, who admits that the whole thing is a misfit and that they would have done better to have ignored it, and hoped for better cards next hand.

'I was *sure* you must have had something,' says dummy sadly.

c

Exposure Penitent

It was a reasonable assumption, but, as Brutus put it, there are no tricks in plain and simple faith.

A good dummy is usually worth an over-trick or two, not merely by exercising his rights (more about that later), but by confusing the defence in the mere act of laying out his hand. Apart from setting out the cards upside down—that is, with the highest cards at the bottom of the row, so that dummy's hand appears to dummy as it ought to look to declarer—it is always a good idea to put the two rows of red suits together and the two black suits together. And by not putting the trump suit in its traditional position on the extreme left of dummy facing declarer, but in the second row with its matching coloured suit in the first row, you can usually cause a certain amount of confusion to the opposition.

And to declarer as well, of course. I have known a declarer play half a hand convinced that Diamonds were trumps when in reality it was Hearts—a fact of life he learned only when, after drawing two rounds of what he thought were trumps, one of his opponents ran out of Diamonds and smartly put him in his place with a Heart.

More often than not, however, the Colour-Confusion method affects only your opponents, and they are satisfactorily bewildered.

Once West has led and you see dummy for the first time it is most important to lose yourself in thought—that is, after you have greeted dummy's contribution with 'Thank you, partner', 'Oh', 'M'm, I see what you meant about Clubs', or whatever other formal comment you consider the hand merits.

You may or may not learn a lot from this period of

silent contemplation, but it can make quite an impression on the rest of the players—even on dummy, who may well think that your genius will save him from appearing the clot he has been made to feel. There is, however, always the chance that declarer may prove to be an even greater clot.

The deliberate tempo adopted at this opening stage of the game must not be relaxed until after the first card has been played from dummy. If West's lead is up to a singleton on the table, you must hesitate before committing yourself to playing the singleton, holding the card firmly in your fingers on dummy's side of the table, as though to let go of it might earn some penalty or other, while looking from your own hand, back to dummy, back to your own hand, and finally playing the card with all the air of an inspired decision.

The way you play the first trick from dummy will show your opponents what calibre of man you are—far-thinking, forward-looking, able to see the hand as a whole from first to thirteenth trick; but not that you are likely to go two down.

This is because in the process of looking ahead, and planning, like some chess master, what you will do five and six moves after next, you are so obsessed with the brilliant ruffing and finessing you will indulge in at tricks 5 and 6, that you neglect to play the all-important tricks 3 and 4 before them—all-important because that is when you should have been drawing trumps.

When we were younger we were warned that the Embankment was populated entirely by people who had neglected to draw trumps. Since the development of the Welfare State the Embankment has not been quite what it was, and those who did not draw trumps now draw a handsome dole—er, Unemployment Benefit—which, if it is not more than they lost at bridge, is certainly infinitely more than they could ever have won at it. But the principle is the same: failure to draw trumps can have dire results.

While you are deliberating over what to play from dummy on West's opening lead, it is a good thing to have what is known as a Long Cool Look—or, in English, a dekko—at your right-hand neighbour. If he has an impatient and eager look you can place him with more cards than he admitted to in the bidding; if he has a look of boredom and hesitates before playing, pulling first this card, then that, and finally the first card again from his hand, you can probably place him with a worse hand than he claimed in the bidding, a doubleton, or a hand that he should never have mentioned in the bidding at all.

Whoever it was that first said about bridge that you play men, not cards, may have been right—about his kind of bridge. But as far as our kind of bridge is concerned he was only half right, because in Coarse Bridge you have to play your partner, as well as your opponents; *and* his cards.

However, one man's opponent is another man's partner, and the behaviour of your right-hand neighbour as he hesitates and dithers over the card he is to play at trick 1 also has great psychological significance for his partner on your left, who will reach very much the same conclusions about his partner's cards as you do.

Vigilance at the bridge table must never be relaxed, whether you are playing or defending a hand. Your opponents will be watching each other like hawks, and you must never take your eyes off them either. Otherwise you may miss the moment when one of them has exhausted a suit and quietly but noticeably rearranges his hand so that it looks tidy and symmetrical to him.

This rearranging of the cards in mid-hand is an in-grained habit, and though a wife may persuade her husband to give up this public demonstration of the state of his hand for a game or two, he will inevitably revert to it before the evening is out. It is therefore most important to watch out for it.

THE FINESSE

Just as one must expect, and can benefit from, incorrect card-behaviour by opponents, such as the rearranging of cards I have just mentioned (you do it yourself as much as anybody, of course, but it is such a habit by now that you are no longer aware of it), so one must expect, and can suffer from, incorrect card-play by one's opponents.

This is encountered above all in the course of finessing, the success of which depends entirely on the cards being played correctly and conventionally. Let us look at the following situation:

7 6 5

	N		
9 8	W E		A 3 2
	S		

K

In normal circumstances, and in the sort of company where West, East and South have not actually had a look at each other's hands, when the Five is led from North, East as second in hand will play a low card ('second player plays low' is one of the Thousand-and-One-Command-ments of the game). This enables you, sitting in the South position, to make your King in a gentlemanly way—thus, in accordance with the definition of a finesse, 'winning a trick with a card that is not the highest held'.

But in Coarse Bridge, where only a small percentage of the Thousand-and-One Commandments are known, let alone observed, East will as likely as not play the Ace— either because he has a sixth sense, which is unlikely, or because he has decided it is high time he took a trick. Anyway, your quite reasonable hopes of finessing the King are dashed by the ignoramus on your right; which is why you can't really trust anybody, even your opponents, in Coarse Bridge.

Since most Coarse Bridge players are pretty shaky on the whole subject of the finesse, its nature, its purpose and its execution, the unforgivable sin of doing what is called 'finessing against your partner' is committed frequently and always in complete ignorance of what is involved.

There is little one can do about this unfortunate habit except to give an example of it, so that next time the situation arises you will recognise it.

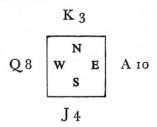

South leads the Jack. West, instead of playing the Queen, as he should, decides to duck and play the Eight. South plays the Three from dummy and East has to take the trick with his Ace. If West had been properly taught in childhood to respect the Commandment 'Thou shalt cover an Honour with an Honour' and had played his Queen, the King would have been played from dummy and East, taking the trick with his Ace, would have left himself with a Ten that was economically viable—in other words good for another trick.

THE SQUEEZE

This is a term one hears a lot from players who have once played bridge in slightly more exalted circles than those in which they find themselves at your table. It is a technical movement which in the ordinary way is unlikely to be used in Coarse Bridge—at least, not consciously. If in the last stages of defending a hand your opponents happen to be faced with the problem of deciding which of their three last cards to discard, they are in the grip of a squeeze, though without knowing it and without your being at all sure how you got them into it.

However, being the players they are, there is no need to give the matter too much thought; they are bound to discard the wrong cards and you'll get credit for subtle 'end' play. When the hand is finished you can do your own bit of name-dropping, as it were, and commiserate with your opponents for having been faced with a merciless squeeze. If, as is likely, they tell you they have never heard the term before you can retort, well, they have now, ha, ha.

Study of what has been described by one of the authorities on Contract Bridge as 'this complex subject' (a description which alone shows how unsuitable it is for you and me) nevertheless introduces us to a term which in the context of Coarse Bridge is an inspired contribution to the vocabulary of the game. This is the term 'One-card

The 'squeeze'

menace'. We need not bother with the role it plays in Squeeze Play, but there was surely never a term that better described the Coarse Bridge player who has a solitary Ace in his hand in No Trumps and is determined to cash it as soon as possible, leaving himself with a fistful of cards any of which, when led, is just what declarer has been waiting for to help him establish his long suits.

There is also, in Squeeze circles, an element known as the 'Two-card menace'. This, too, is found in human form in Coarse Bridge; usually it is your partner, who has a doubleton (or what the French call a *bigleton*, from *bigle*— a squinter*), and invariably gets his signals wrong, playing low-high instead of high-low, and so leading you to suppose that he has his usual quota of humdrum nothings in his hand.

DUMMY AND HIS RIGHTS

Silence is the perfectest herald of joy
SHAKESPEARE

The *Concise Oxford Dictionary* defines dummy as: 'Person taking no real part, or present only for show, figurehead, mere tool, man of straw; dolt, blockhead, sham package, lay figure.'

In spite of the low opinion the dictionary has of him, dummy has many rights which are specified in the laws of the game, and many opportunities for advice and encouragement which are not. It is the latter which deserve most attention for they are not exclusively used by dummy. Coarse Bridge, being a democratic pastime, recognises no privileged classes and the rights enjoyed by

* The opposite of a *bigleton* is a *Lyttelton*.

dummy are shared by all. Dummy himself, apart from being officially entitled 'to draw attention to any irregularity or to warn his partner against committing any irregularity such as revoking or leading from the wrong hand', frequently reminds declarer of facts which seem to be slipping his memory by asking questions like 'What did Sally bid after Brian passed?' This will elicit information that suggests that Sally must have a King that declarer ought to know about. Another question is 'Having no Ace, partner?' when declarer carelessly plays a card that can lose him an unnecessary trick.

Dummy's game is one that three can play, and the opposition will naturally join in with their own helpful questions, answers and observations. The nature of these interpolations, however, will be discussed in the section on Defensive Play where they rightly belong.

Dummy can also neatly provoke his opponents into some punishable irregularities if he is careful. Right at the start of the game, before the first card has been led, he can manœuvre the conversation in such a way that East may be persuaded to ask 'My lead is it?' Dummy will say in a quiet aside that it is. East leads to be told that he has led out of turn. His card stays on the table, dummy is spread out, South tells West what to lead, West is furious with East, South and North smile slyly.

This tactic is usually worth an overtrick or two, but should not be tried too often against the same opponents.

Finally, there is one right which dummy does not share with the rest of the table, and that is the right to look at his partner's cards when his own hand is first exposed. Dummy's reaction to the sight of his partner's hand can have a considerable psychological effect on opponents. A subdued wolf-whistle that clearly says 'My word!' can demoralise the opposition into accepting defeat from a hand in a million almost before a card has been played; and a bad-tempered, contemptuous snort of 'Mph!' or 'Pshaw!' can lull them into a sense of false security, which will cause them to make silly mistakes in their over-confidence.

DEFENSIVE PLAY

> Then dreams he of smelling out a suit
>
> SHAKESPEARE

There are some who may laugh at the optimism of an old lady I know of who, when her opponents won the first game of the rubber, would address her partner joyfully with 'Now, partner, we've got them vulnerable!'

But it is not as ridiculous as it may seem on first thoughts. From the defender's point of view vulnerable opponents mean extra points to be gained from putting them down, and it is the defender's aim to put them down as profitably as possible.

Unless they have passed throughout the bidding the defenders will have learned what little they know about each other's hand from the course of the auction. If neither of them has been able to call there is bound to be a time during the play of the hand when West, for instance, may be a little unsure (to coin an understatement) what to lead. At this point he should casually ask the assembled company what trumps are. East will quickly reply Hearts, which is immediately contradicted by his opponents who are playing Four Spades. West, however, now knows that he should lead a Heart.

Perhaps this little charade may strike some as rather shady practice, if not actually cheating; in that case let me assure them that the subtle nuances of Coarse Bridge are pure as the driven snow compared with the signalling, table-rapping, voice-inflexions, cigarette-lighting, kicks under the table and different ways of holding cards that go on between partners at some bridge clubs during the bidding as well as during the hand.

The practice I have described may, I think, seem less reprehensible to toffee-nosed moralists who play only patience (and are suspiciously successful in always making it come out), when I emphasise the importance of the end to which it is a means. More friendships and marriages have foundered on the rocks of the calling card ignored or misunderstood in defensive play than in any other way, and it is to guard against this eternally threatening disaster that what one might call the False Trump Query is introduced.

It must be stressed that this action is taken only in desperation—that is, when inspiration has finally run dry and other more orthodox means have failed. It is a sure-fire life-saver in a tight spot, however. It also has the advantage of being extremely simple.

The experts, if they can possibly avoid it, will never make things simple for the amateur. This is necessary for them if there is to be any future in writing bridge books for beginners; if things were kept simple there'd be nothing to explain.

Take what is known as the Rule of Eleven, for instance. The very mention of eleven suggests the occult, where the numbers seven and eleven have great mystic significance, and the Coarse Bridge player may get the born gambler's glint in his eye when he hears about it. Unfortunately, all the Rule of Eleven does is involve you in a lot of mental arithmetic that can land you in a terrible muddle.

The Rule of Eleven applies only to a hand played in No

Trumps, and is intended to make the play easier for the defenders—or rather, for one of the defenders, East. The Rule is so called because the cards in the pack rank in value from 2 to 14 (the top four cards, Jack, Queen, King, Ace, have faces instead of pips, except the Ace, which has one pip and beats the lot).

If, as his opening lead, West plays the fourth highest of his longest suit he should have three cards higher than that left in the suit. This number, 3, subtracted from 14 leaves 11. Q.—I suppose—E. D.

Having learnt this equation East then starts doing sums in earnest. All East can see at West's lead is:

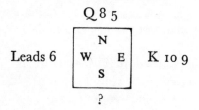

West leads the Six. East then subtracts 6 (the value of West's card) from 11, which leaves 5. He then takes away two from dummy—the two cards which are higher than the Six—and three from his own, which are all higher than the Six. According to this reckoning 11-6-2-3=0. Therefore declarer, whom nobody has mentioned so far, but whose strength in the suit East and West and probably dummy (out of sheer inquisitiveness) want to know, has no card in the suit higher than the Six led by West. If this is so then dummy no doubt wonders how they're going to do in Three No Trumps.

The Rule of Eleven can also be applied by East (if he has the time as well as a pencil and paper for his sums) to find out whether, instead of playing the fourth highest of his longest suit, West isn't perhaps playing the 'top of nothing'. East takes 6 from 11 and gets the answer 5; however, the five cards higher than West's Six are all visible—in dummy and in East's own hand. Therefore declarer, who had no cards worth mentioning the first time the data were fed into the computer, is now shown as likely to have Ace, Jack and Seven. Or not.

East, being probably none the wiser after his excursions into higher mathematics, is now best advised to study his partner's facial expression, which may give him more of a clue to the reason for his lead of the Six than any Rule of Eleven. If yon partner has a lean and hungry look, it is quite possible that he just wishes it was dinner time and has led his Six for no other reason than that he couldn't think of any card less likely to cause trouble, have any significance, or otherwise hold up the game. After all, reasons West, there must be *some* cards that don't mean a damned thing.

Whether this lead is popular with his partner or not is another matter. It is one of the advantages of our sort of bridge that East can show his feelings in ways far more eloquent than the rather naive one of playing a high card as a signal to come on. Owing to the way in which bridge and chess articles in the Sunday newspapers are nearly always printed in adjoining columns, many readers find themselves confused by the presence of Kings and Queens in both places, and references to systems of defence that might apply to either game. Many Coarse Bridge players who have read the chess articles by mistake have adapted some famous defences to suit their bridge.

In chess everybody knows the Sicilian Defence and the French Defence. There are a growing number of Coarse Bridge players who now use these terms to describe newly evolved defensive tactics. The most popular is the French

Defence, which consists of greeting your partner's welcome opening lead with the words '*Oo-la-la*' spoken in a gloomy tone of voice which he will correctly interpret as signifying approval and encouragement. The unwelcome lead is received with a delighted cry of '*Zut! alors!*', which may seem to your opponents a sound of rejoicing. Your partner, on the other hand, having looked up the word *Zut* in a French-English dictionary, will recognise it as a popular interjection expressing vexation, spite, contempt, scorn or indifference. After reference to a French-English dictionary your partner will know that *Zut* can in one word mean 'You be blowed!', 'You be hanged!', 'Confound it!', 'Hang it!', 'I'm not going to do it!', 'Not I!', 'Stuff!', 'Not a bit of it!', 'It's no use!', 'It's no go!', 'I give it up!', and with unanswerable finality 'Goodbye!' A versatile word, one must admit.

The Sicilian Defence, like the French Defence, again makes use of inflexions intended to convey to the opposition the exact opposite of what it means to the defence. A good lead by West is encouraged by East with a resigned, long-drawn-out '*Dio!*' (pronounced 'Deeeeeeoh!'), accompanied by a slow and emphatic shrug of the shoulders and a helpless raising of the hands. The bad lead is received with '*Bravo, bravissimo!*', or, if West is a woman, with the carefully correct '*Brava, bravissima!*'

Whatever West's sex, however, they will not be spared the characteristic Sicilian strokes that go with the words; these are known as the *pedata d'amore*, which is a short, sharp kick on the shin, and the *calpestata*, which is a carefully applied pressure of the foot on partner's toes if you can reach them.

An important and rarely discussed aspect of Defensive Play is the action that the defenders must take to remind some cocky declarers of their manners. The need for this

French defence

arises when declarer can see the last five or six tricks clearly and begins to play them out at a speed which is madly irritating and impolite. In an almost simultaneous movement South plays his own card and one from dummy. This habit can be so infuriating to the opposition that I have known it to break up a marriage. South's husband, having had to defend a hand played in this way as East once too often, finally left her and married West.

The only answer to this break-neck tempo is for the defence to take their time, insisting very deliberately that dummy's card, if only as a courtesy, shall not be played before West has played. West will go into a trance while he considers what to play, fingering first this card, then that, pulling a card out, holding it over the table without exposing it, putting it back, then finally playing it after all. East repeats the routine, even more slowly if possible.

After a couple of tricks South will in desperation claim that all the rest are there, and will lay down her hand. East and West concede nothing, and insist on playing the hand. Their action will not cure these habitual speed hogs, but it can keep them in their place.

For all the good the bridge articles usually do them, those who wish to perfect the art of Defensive Play in Coarse Bridge are probably better off reading the chess columns in any case. In this way they can save themselves the sort of headache that is caused by trying to sort out the philosophy and reasoning of the following essay on tic-tac which once appeared in the *Sunday Times*:

On the King of Spades lead East drops the Ten and the declarer the Queen. What message is East trying to convey? Normally a high card demands a continuation of the suit. It can also show two or four, but why the Ten? Can the declarer's Queen be a false card? The answer is no, he would hardly bid

Five Clubs with three Spades to the Queen. He would be more likely to try Three No Trumps. So the message must be different.

East must be indicating four Spades, but the exceptionally high card must also indicate the Ace of Hearts . . .

. . . And what message did East send to his partner at Trick 1? The Ten of Spades said 'Partner, I have four Spades, I do not think you have the Ace, King, Queen, or you would have bid One Spade. If you have only four then cash another. I have the Ace of Hearts, but if you switch immediately I shall be in doubt whether to give you a ruff or try to cash a second Spade. Had I held five Spades I would have played my lowest one.'

Which just shows what the late Kenneth Konstam meant when in the course of that article he said: 'There is also a *language* of defence.'

As for you and me, if we could read all that into a simple Ten of Spades we wouldn't need to try to make money playing bridge. We could make a million telling fortunes on fairgrounds.

4   *Ethics and Customs*

What custom wills, in all things we should do't
SHAKESPEARE

AT this point I would like to touch on the historical background of the Coarse Bridge movement.

The great schism in the Bridge World, as far-reaching in its effect on the human race as the French Revolution and the discovery of alcohol, took place on a day in December 1929 when the Portland Club promulgated the first code of laws to govern Contract Bridge.

One glance at these and it was obvious that secession was inevitable if the game, indeed the human spirit itself, were not to be stifled by fascist repression, and the rights of the individual to freedom of speech and action were not to perish from the earth.

The Coarse Bridge movement, following in the true tradition of other organised British labour, regarded itself as unwarrantably insulted by the innuendoes and implications contained in the Laws of Contract Bridge. What kind of people did the Portland Club think we were that their laws should include a section headed 'Proprieties' and divided into such sub-sections as 'Violations of Ethical Conduct' and 'Observance of Proper Etiquette'?

Did they imagine we were the sort who would ever make a remark, gesture, mannerism or question which might convey information to partner, or might mislead an opponent? That we would ever show approval or disapproval of partner's call or—of all things!—satisfaction with an opponent's call?

Or that we were so ill-bred that we had to be told to maintain a courteous attitude towards our partner and opponents, carefully avoiding any remark or action which might cause annoyance or embarrassment to another player, or might interfere with the enjoyment of the game?

And as for looking intently at any other player during the auction or play periods, or at another player's hand for the purpose of observing the place from which he draws a card—what sort of company does the Portland Club keep that an infamous suggestion of this kind has to be included in their sanctimonious epilogue to the laws of the game? Even the Laws of Cricket, which permit more underhand but strictly legal ways of defeating or inconveniencing an opponent than those of any other game, do not have to legislate for the unutterable cad and bounder.

But the Portland Club's directions and admonitions did not end with insulting the player; they insulted the spectator as well. As if it was not enough to tell players to refrain during play from making gratuitous remarks about the auction or the adequacy of the contract, from exchanging hands with their partners or letting their partners see their hands, from indicating expectation or intention of winning or losing a trick before the trick has been completed—as if all this could be taken lying down by any player with an atom of self-respect and pride in him, the Laws of Contract Bridge tell the spectator that he should refrain from gratuitous remarks or mannerisms of any kind and not call attention to any irregularity or mistake, or speak unless he is spoken to.

Obviously a very thin-skinned lot, those serious

bridgeurs, and inordinately touchy, that they should keep harping on 'gratuitous' comments and 'gratuitous' remarks. Did they expect a claque to make called-for comments and remarks perhaps?

What added further insult to the dictatorial, not to say 'gratuitous', insinuations contained in the official laws was the support given to them (with interest) by bridge writers in the innumerable booklets which appeared at the same time. In one of these, published in the early 1930s and called *Contract Bridge While You Wait*, or some such title that would hardly pass the Trade Descriptions laws of today, the author has an admonitory list of 'Don'ts' which includes the following:

(1) 'Don't look at your opponents' cards. It prevents you from claiming a revoke.'

Well! I must say this is as cynical a reason for not looking at your opponents' cards as ever I heard. You mustn't look at your opponents' cards, not because it is dishonest, but because if there were a revoke you couldn't claim it. For ourselves, we would willingly forgo the opportunity of claiming a revoke for a good butcher's at the opposition's cards, and according to the reasoning of the author of these 'Don'ts', we would be quite entitled to. (As a side-thought: there must have been an awful lot of revoking in those early days if it paid you so well not to lose the privilege of claiming a revoke. Whether they were all colour blind or had never been taught the ritual of following suit, I do not know; but every other page of those bridge books of the 1930s has something to say on the matter.)

The list of 'Don'ts' continues:

(2) 'Don't emphasise a bid, pass, double or play.'

(3) 'Don't hesitate in bidding.'

(4) 'Don't criticise your partner.'

(5) 'Don't call attention to the score.'

(6) 'Don't grumble at your luck.'

(7) 'Don't hold inquests.'

(8) 'Don't fidget when dummy.'

Taking them one by one:

(2) How can you get your partner to take any notice unless you do emphasise a bid, pass, double or play?

(3) The alternative to hesitation in bidding is to say the first thing that comes into your head. Is this seriously recommended?

(4) If *you* don't criticise your partner, who the hell will?

(5) What score?

(6) Why not?

(7) Another blow by the Executive against freedom of speech. If you can't hold an inquest, what on earth is anybody to talk about between hands?

(8) 'Don't fidget when dummy.' But the advice goes on: 'Watch the play and check up on opponents, particularly when they do not follow suit'. This seems a little illogical; after denying yourself the right in Don't No. 1 of looking at your opponents' cards because to do so would prevent you claiming a revoke, what is the point of stopping your opponents revoking? And what does 'check up on your opponents' mean? Do you warn them, tell on them, send their dossier to Interpol, or what? It is enough to make any dummy fidget.

In view of all the threats to individual liberty, the 'gratuitous' insults, innuendoes and back-handers they contained, it was clearly impossible for the Coarse Bridge movement to accept the newly promulgated Laws of Contract Bridge in 1929. Nailing their declaration of independence on the doors of the Portland Club, the heroes of the resistance arose and, greeting their excom-

munication with some rather rude gestures and mannerisms, lit a candle that has burned happily ever after.

Not only was the whole tone and tenor of the Laws of
Contract Bridge intolerable, embodying as they did
tyrannical circumscriptions that amounted to no less
than persecution of a minority, but if the Laws were
observed it would be altogether impossible to enjoy a
decent game of bridge at all.

And that, comrades and fellow workers, is why Coarse
Bridge has its own strict code of Ethics, and its uniquely
tolerant Customs.

Study of the Ethics of the game is not an involved or
lengthy undertaking, for in essence the Ethical Code is
based quite simply on the exact opposite of that shown in
the Laws I have mentioned. This is not to say that the
ethics of Coarse Bridge do not include some pretty peculiar
and profound thoughts—that is to say, pretty profound
thoughts that are peculiar to our Way of Life. One of
them is the first, basic rule that mistakes must always be
accepted philosophically, especially your own; the more
disastrous your mistake has been, the more platitudinous
must be your comment—'Never mind, it'll all be the
same in a hundred years' time'; or 'While there's life
there's hope'; or 'Tomorrow's another day'. There are
worse ones than these, if you can remember them, and
all of them are apt.

The trouble about so many of the proscriptions occurring
in the Laws is that, like the Law of Blasphemy, their
justice is entirely a matter of opinion. But, as Bernard
Shaw said, all great truths began as blasphemies; and if
the Coarse Bridge movement is based on anything, it is
on great truths.

Ethics

INTERPRETATION OF THE LAWS

Frustrate their knavish tricks

OLD SONG

The Laws of Coarse Bridge, like those of Coarse Cricket, are nothing if not flexible. They are founded on what may be thought a rather libertarian principle—namely, that all Coarse Bridge players are born pretty mediocrely equal and that if one player wants to detach a card from his hand before it is his turn to lead or play, he is at liberty to do so, as long as what goes for him goes for everyone else at the table.

Where laws are not broken, penalties do not arise. In this way we are spared the business of penalty cards being left face upwards on the table like children being made to stand in a corner, of players being obliged to pass next time it is their turn to call like children being kept in after school, to play this suit or to be prohibited from leading that. If by any awful chance a player should mistakenly come to our table who so far misunderstands our ethics and customs as to demand a penalty for any trivial breach of the Laws, such as a revoke, his appeal is ignored, his opponents are awarded a bonus of 60 points (20 above the line and 40 below), he forfeits a hundred honours if he has them, 10 points are deducted from all minor suit tricks he may have made, and 20 from all major suit tricks and No Trumps, and he is never invited again.

For this is the sort of player who digs up an Act of 1603 (1 & 36 Jac. I c. 178) to deny dummy's right to inquire into revokes and point out and stop irregularities, if he (dummy) swops hands with the declarer, looks over declarer's shoulder when he plays, or looks at the cards in either opponent's hand unless invited to do so. People who invoke a law like that have to pay the supreme penalty of going without the dinner that dummy—among her other social acts mentioned above and performed in accordance with Magna Carta and the First Amendment —has been cooking for him.

COSTUME AND EQUIPMENT

Nothing divides the various grades of bridge more sharply than the difference in the kind of costume and equipment considered proper to them.

At one end of the scale we have the fancy hats and pearls of the women's afternoon bridge clubs, where the players seem to be in a permanent state of either just going to or just coming from a cocktail party. At the other, we have the indescribable informality and infinite variety of the clothes worn where Coarse Bridge is played, whose characteristic colour and comfort are in themselves as unmistakably peculiar as any uniform.

The afternoon club table is laid with new packs of cards not yet hatched from their cellophane egg shells, the excise stamps still unbroken; neat little newly sharpened pencils peep from pockets of tidy blank score pads. On our table there are the same old packs, stained and dog-eared, with the Six of Spades and Four of Clubs (or is it the King of Diamonds and the Ace of Hearts?) still clearly identifiable by the marks of rough red Algerian wine spilt over them in the days when it was five shillings a bottle. The scoring pads still bear the scribbled and corrected figures of the last rubber played, and before the end of the evening at least one pad will run out and have to be replaced by sheets of expensive typewriting paper divided into halves.

The reason for the rather inadequate state of the equipment used in Coarse Bridge is that *because* one plays Coarse Bridge one is denied—or, rather, spared—the annual gifts of bridge gear which players of classier bridge are given regularly by nephews and nieces at Christmas. In our house, thank goodness, we have long been able to proclaim willingness to receive, as Christmas presents from younger relations, boxes of very special and exceedingly expensive French soap. These (and here is a household tip thrown in for free) are dated and laid down, not to be used for a year. If the soap is allowed to harden and mature it lasts much longer when you eventually come to use it, and it doesn't lose its scent. We certainly wouldn't consider suggesting that packs of cards and scorers should ever take its place.

Once in a decade or so, one of our friends, unable any longer to bear the state of the cards we play with, will arrive for an evening's bridge bringing a brand-new couple of packs as a gift. The gesture is accepted with at any rate an outward show of gratitude, and the new cards are used that very evening—a little reluctantly, at least at first, because they are strange to us.

But they are not strange for long; after half a dozen rubbers or so the new cards, stained with today's rough red Algerian wine at today's inflated prices, are barely distinguishable from the old set. The only real difference between them is that in the newer pack the cards we soon come to recognise immediately by their wine markings are the King of Diamonds and the Ace of Hearts (or is it the Six of Spades and the Four of Clubs?).

The advantages of playing as many Coarse Bridge fixtures as possible at home will, I hope, be apparent from the above, and the experienced player will arrange things accordingly. On away fixtures he can be faced with

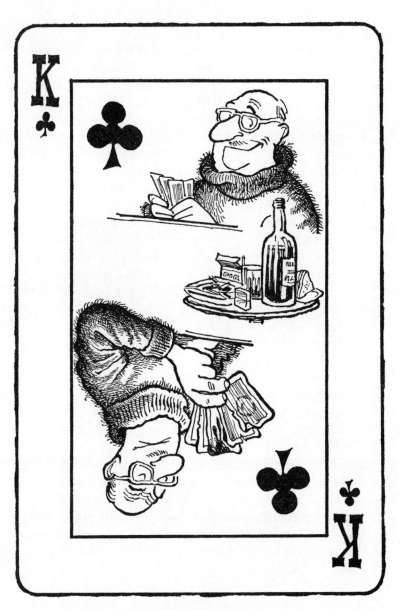

Costume and Equipment

entirely strange cards, the back of every one of which looks exactly the same to him. This is a situation a player must try to avoid by clever planning and imaginative excuses—insisting that he has a new, interesting little wine he wants to try out with his friends, pretending that he is being troubled by his old war wound (the one he sustained when he was digging his garden seven years ago and the wheelbarrow tipped over on his foot), claiming that it is *his* turn to be host and that the car is being serviced anyway.

That the net profit at the end of a home fixture, even at £0·01 or One New Penny a hundred, is not enough to pay for the detergent used in washing up after your guests have left is immaterial. It is the principle that counts—the principle and the simple pleasure of winning at cards, for, as Othello put it, 'They laugh that win'.

Sometimes, anyway.

The equipment needed for Coarse Bridge includes more than cards, score-pads and a folding table that doesn't collapse. It includes small tables to put at the players' elbows, glasses to put on the tables, and drinks to put in the glasses. The provision of all these never gives us any trouble.

What we are always forgetting, however, is that whereas we do not smoke, other people do, and that we ought to provide cigarettes and ashtrays. Cigarettes we sometimes manage, when we have remembered to bring back the permitted number of duty-free cartons from the boat on returning from our holidays in September; but they are pretty stale by the end of the Coarse Bridge season in April.

But while people nearly always bring their own cigarettes, they rarely bring their own ashtrays. Every home bridge fixture involves us in a house-wide search for suitable receptacles to hold the mess and indestructible debris of the modern filter-tip cigarette. In the end we succeed in restoring a number of heavy glass objects used as door-stoppers, and bowls filled with paper clips, to their original use as ashtrays.

As a postscript: For anybody who cares to try it, I recommend the method I used to give up smoking as long ago as 1954. My own consumption of cigarettes had been seventy to eighty a day, until I had a very bad cold, so bad that I couldn't smoke at all. While I had the cold I reminded myself of how peculiarly nasty the first cigarette after a cold had always tasted. The prospect of that first cigarette was so unpleasant that I never had it. My cold left me and I found I had lost the taste for tobacco altogether. One really couldn't pine for a cigarette one knew was going to taste like old hay soaked in liquorice. It was as easy as that.

EXCUSES AND EXPLANATIONS

You have done that you should be sorry for
SHAKESPEARE

However much the experts (see p. 83) may hope to persuade you to the contrary, the inquest or post mortem is to Coarse Bridge what the hurly-burly of Question Time is to Parliament.

It is only after a hand has been played that any of the play can be openly discussed at length (mid-play discussions tend to be interrupted by impatient opponents who want to get on with the game). While the debate is usually monopolised by the losers, one of whom accuses the other of not having led a particular card which would not have made a tittle of difference to the result, the winners are just as likely to be heard arguing over the way they ought to have bid the Six Clubs they made instead of leaving it in Four Clubs, which didn't even give them game.

This is the time, too, when both sides learn a lot about the conventions they think they have been playing, and are able to reproach their partners for misleading them.

The root of the trouble very often lies in the fact that a little reading is a dangerous thing. I don't mean just reading the Laws (though this is reprehensible enough in its tendency to turn some people into busybodies with ideas above their bridge-playing station), but the bridge articles which give the reader of the Quality Newspapers good advice mixed with hair-raising cautionary anecdote.

It is the casual glance at one of these that can lead the Coarse Bridge player into a jungle of cross-purposes that not even the most carefully conducted inquest will disentangle. There is, for instance, the Roman Club convention which happened to catch the eye of one of our companions recently. Without warning his partner that he intended to use it, or even explaining what it was, South found himself playing One Club with this hand, which West, North and East had all passed:

S: Q 10 4
H: Q 10 6
D: Q 10 8 3
C: 9 6 2

S: K 7   S: J 9 6 3 2
H: 7 4 3 2   N   H: 9 8
D: 6 5   W   E   D: 7 4 2
C: K J 8 7 3   S   C: A 5 4

S: A 8 5
H: A K J 5
D: A K J 9
C: Q 10

West led a trump, taken with the Ace by East, who returned a small Club, and West, for all the world as if he were the declarer, proceeded to draw trumps, making four more Club tricks and eventually the King of Spades. South made his contract of One Club. Just. Dummy congratulated him, muttering as he put down the score:

'One Club, as bid: 20 points.'

The dialogue that now followed was a touch acrimonious. Didn't dummy recognise the Roman Club when he heard it? No, he'd never heard of it until that moment. The Two Club, the Indian Club, the Neapolitan Club, yes—but not the Roman Club. He supposed there'd be a Palermo Club next.

Patiently South explained that the Roman Club, brilliantly exploited by the great Italian world champions, meant that he had either a minimum balanced hand or a very strong one.

'Which did you have?' asked dummy.

'That isn't the point,' replied South. 'You shouldn't have passed.'

'Why not? I hadn't anything to bid about.'

'You should have kept it open.'

'Why, if you had only a minimum balanced hand?'

'I had a very strong hand.'

'How was I to know that?'

'Because I was playing the Roman Club.'

'I see.' Dummy paused, and went on: 'How was I to keep it open?'

D

'By bidding One Diamond. That's the negative response.'

'Just like Vanderbilt.'

'Who's Vanderbilt, may I ask?'

'Oh, don't you know?' (Dummy had done a little reading too—once.) 'Vanderbilt was a famous convention. You opened One Club to show three Quick Tricks. And One Diamond was the negative—less than two Quick Tricks.'

'Then what?'

'I imagine you hoped your opponents would say something.'

'What if you wanted to play it in Clubs?'

'You'd have to say Two Clubs over One Diamond.'

'And have to make Two Clubs when you only wanted One?'

'Yes. You could make an overtrick that way.'

'Or not?'

'Or not.'

'The Portland Club posted a notice or something,' dummy continued, warming to his subject, 'asking their members please to refrain from using Vanderbilt. They said it prevented people bidding One ordinary Club; and besides, it was—and I quote— "utterly mechanical and contrary to all British instincts of fair play", no less.'

'I should think so, too,' said North emphatically. 'You can't have a Forcing One convention.'

'Like the Roman Club, for instance,' suggested West, quietly.

'That's different. Everybody understands that convention,' said South.

'We didn't,' said East.

'Nor did I,' said dummy. 'You didn't give anybody any warning.'

'Well, what do you suggest?' asked South impatiently.

'Sing a verse of "Arrivederci Roma"—words and music,' said West.

'Don't know them,' grumbled South.

'That's the idea,' said dummy; and the conversation turned to other things.

Then there was the case of the Unusual No Trump which somebody once read about. As nearly all No Trump bids in Coarse Bridge are not only unusual but asking for trouble, it was a bold innovation indeed to introduce something actually known officially as the Unusual No Trump, especially without warning.

To be fair, a freakish bid like that (it sounds like the title of a detective story) was not out of keeping with the freakish hands it was bid against.

```
        S: A K Q J 10 7 6 4
        H: Q 4
        D: ———————————
        C: Q 7 6

S: 3 2          ┌─────────┐      S: 9
H: 10 6         │    N    │      H: 7
D: A K 7 3 2    │ W     E │      D: Q J 9 8 6 5
C: 9 8 4 3      │    S    │      C: A K J 5 2
                └─────────┘
        S: 8 5
        H: A K J 9 8 5 3 2
        D: 10 4
        C: 10
```

South dealt and opened Four Hearts. North answered with Six Spades. East then opened his mouth for the first time and called Six (unusual, not to say unexpected) No Trumps.

There was a significant pause in the proceedings at this point. It seems that East wanted to know what was West's better minor suit. Fortunately for East and West South intervened and bid Seven Hearts. If South had passed, West would have had to say Seven Diamonds, which would have been doubled and defeated. The most likely consequence, however, would have been that West, being as puzzled as his opponents by what East was up to, would have passed and North would have bid Seven Spades. He wouldn't have made it, of course, any more than South should have made the Seven Hearts the hand was eventually played in: in either case East and West can defeat the contract by making the correct lead of a Club. As it was, West led his Ace of Diamonds and the contract was made without trouble.

At the inquest it was agreed that the Unusual No Trump, while an interesting call, was not very profitable unless backed up by a Usual, or at any rate an Intelligent, opening lead. Nobody seemed to know the purpose of the Unusual No Trump, unless it was to push North and South into a grand slam which they couldn't make with a Club lead. What was never explained was what would have happened if East had been left in Six No Trumps—which might well have happened as West obviously didn't know what his partner was supposed to be talking about. It's possible that his partner didn't know either.

Finally, it is advisable to remember at all inquests and Boards of Enquiry that attack is the best defence against your partner's complaints. Get in quick with: 'If you hadn't played the Ten instead of the Eight . . .'

'I didn't have the Eight.'

'Well, whatever it was. If you hadn't played the Ten we'd have put them down.'

This method, with any luck, will divert your partner from his intention to raise hell about your stupid failure to return his lead of a singleton. Or at least delay the introduction of this topic long enough for your opponents to intervene and demand that the rubber should continue.

EXCUSES AND EXPLANATIONS (cont.)
SOME USEFUL PHRASES

Vain denial and coy excuse

MILTON

THE DECLARER
After obstinately bidding up to Five Diamonds against his partner's Clubs on a bare One Diamond hand and going four down: 'You should have left me in Two Diamonds, partner.'

After obstinately bidding up to Five Diamonds against his partner's Clubs on a bare One Diamond hand and going four down: 'I'm afraid it was a misfit, partner.'

After obstinately bidding up to Five Diamonds against his partner's Clubs on a bare One Diamond hand and seeing dummy for the first time: 'If you'd shown your Clubs, partner, we could have made Three No Trumps on our ear.'

On going six down, vulnerable against opponents who were not, in a small slam, doubled and redoubled: 'Never mind, partner, we stopped them getting a game.'

On making Six Spades doubled against an opponent with two Aces in his hand, and not redoubling: 'I shall not pass that way again.'

DUMMY
Having overbid: 'I was only keeping it open.'

Ditto: 'You always manage to make it somehow, so I thought we'd have a go at game.'

Ditto: 'You know I'm a gambler, partner.'

Ditto: 'Having had no cards all evening I'm afraid they rather went to my head.'

Ditto: 'I haven't got anything, partner. I was just defending the rubber.'

Ditto: 'I haven't got anything, partner. I just didn't see why they should get away with it.'

Ditto: 'I haven't got anything, partner, but I knew you wouldn't mind.'

Ditto: 'I only called Four Hearts to finish the rubber.'

Ditto and displaying a Yarborough: 'I know you always play a strong No Trump, so I was sure you'd make Three with this.'

After declarer has suffered blood, toil and tears to scrape home with One Diamond: 'Well done. That's all we needed.'

On putting down a hand with One doubtful Quick Trick which he has been confidently upping to a slam: 'I felt you must have something.'

On putting down a hand with no Quick Tricks at all, but which he has nevertheless supported declarer with: 'I shan't mind if you go one down, partner.'

Ditto: 'How could I tell you were reverse bidding?'

To her husband: 'I know you didn't want to be left in One No Trump, darling, but I've got to go and dish up the dinner.'

THE DEFENDERS

On doubling South into game: 'He always overbids. I doubled on principle.'

When partner leads a singleton and asks why you didn't return the suit: 'I didn't want to waste your trumps.'

On being asked by partner why he didn't take any notice of his high-low signalling: 'As they were both losers, I thought it was just coincidence which you pulled out first.'

Excuses and Explanations

On being asked by partner why he persisted in playing his Clubs when a Heart had been called for: 'Well, as it was No Trumps I knew I'd make the Three of Clubs in the end.'

Ditto: 'I thought it was a discard—you know: throwing a loser on a loser and all that.'

On being told he has finessed against his partner: 'Oh, did I? How?'

On being reprimanded for leading the lowest, not the fourth highest, of his longest suit in No Trumps: 'Don't you know a False Card when you see one? "A card intended to deceive, usually a card that departs from convention"?'

After doubling Six Spades with two Aces in his hand and failing to break the contract: 'How was I to know he had a blank suit?'

Ditto: 'Well, anyway, partner, they didn't redouble.'

On trumping partner's Ace: 'Sorry, partner, no alternative. Luck of the draw, you know.'

On not trumping partner's Ace: 'Trump your Ace? You won't catch me with *that* old music-hall joke.'

On having one's Ace trumped by partner: 'Luck of the draw, my foot! You just haven't been paying attention.'

On not having one's Ace trumped by partner: 'Good God, man, how do you expect to get into your own hand otherwise?'

5

Last Hand

And a quiet sleep and a sweet dream when the long
trick's over
MASEFIELD

IF there is one virtue more than another that distinguishes the true Coarse Bridge player, it is his stead-
fastness of character and his unswerving adherence both
to his own principles and to those of all who sail with
him.

Constant attempts are made in a subtle, not to say
insidious, way by propagandists of Higher Bridge to
seduce him from the ethical standards and technical
pleasures he enjoys as a true amateur of his chosen and
cherished pastime.

'Why not,' the voice of temptation whispers in your
ear, 'why not extend your playing circle? Why always
play with the family? Why not go out and about
into the great bridge world and do things and meet
people?'

Why not indeed? Except that you can't think of
anybody outside the family, and all the security and
friendly affection the term implies, who would ever invite
you to play bridge with them. And if they did, how is one
to be sure one would want to play with them?

It would involve reconsidering one's entire deportment
at the bridge table—the way to hold the cards, the way
to look at stern and unfamiliar partners, the tone of

voice—one's whole tenor and demeanour, in fact. This must lead inevitably to loss of concentration on the game and deterioration of morale, enthusiasm and enjoyment.

No! In Coarse Bridge, East is East and West is West, and never the twain shall meet as partners at any table where they cannot behave as they do in their own drawing room.

We must stand like Horatius and keep our Bridge, with one to sit on our right hand, and one to sit on our left side, and a dummy in his usual place opposite. For the attacks and attempted infiltrations are unceasing, and at least one generation of bridge players in every family will try to undermine your delight in the Goulash, because 'it isn't bridge'. But Coarse Bridge isn't bridge either, thank goodness, and that is why the Goulash still continues to flourish in the best circles.

The tradition of the Goulash, it had better be explained, goes back to the very first years of Contract Bridge, and we find in a booklet on conventions written in 1931 a discussion of 'pre-emptive' bidding which includes the following:

'Holding a suit of great length and top strength, and weak side cards, the bidder . . . may even pass originally and enter the bidding later, possibly to greater advantage.' The author of the booklet adds his comment in brackets: ['especially in Goulashes'].

This is the only reference to Goulashes in the book, so they seem to have been a pretty widely accepted practice that needed no explanation.

A book on Contract Bridge for beginners published a year earlier, in its section of 'General Information' on such things as Two-Suited Hands, Rule of Eleven, Unblocking, Slam Bidding, the Vanderbilt Convention and the like, includes as its final and longest item a description of Goulashes.

There are several forms, the book says, none of them legal—the latter a quality which at once endears the idea of the Goulash to the libertarian, anti-establishment instincts of the Coarse Bridge player. Without indicating precisely when a Goulash is played (according to common modern practice it is introduced at the stage when all four players are tired of having to throw in a whole series of unbiddable hands), the section gives instructions on how to deal for it. When all four players have arranged their unbiddable cards tidily in graded suits, South the dealer places his hand on the table, East places his hand on top of it, North puts his on top of East's, and West finally crowns the stack with his. The cards are then straightened and cut. The dealer deals out five cards at a time to each player, then another five, and then a final three.

If there is a misdeal a penalty of 100 points can be claimed—a nice touch by the inventor of the Goulash, who foresaw that few players would be practised in the skills of dealing cards in fives, fives and threes, and that those who weren't might be a source of revenue to half the players at the table.

Goulashes, however, are optional, the book continued. If one player objects, Goulashes cannot be played. Ignoring this possibility—as though anybody one played with would be such a po-faced spoil-sport— we come to two more methods of distributing cards for a Goulash.

In these cases the Goulash is not 'dealt', but after a pass all round and a decision to play a Goulash, the players keep their hands. The first method is the exchange of cards between partners: they swap three, then two, then one. A singleton in the first three shows the suit the donor requires. If the singleton is a six or higher, you don't have to start doing sums about the Rule of Eleven; it means he has the Ace.

The other form is a variation of this method—partners exchange one, then three, then two cards. The single card first passed is to show the suit required. If a high honour is passed you must return it; if both partners want the same suit, the player receiving the highest honour keeps it.

Both these forms sound so like some nightmare cross between Cribbage, Happy Families and Old Maid that I feel it must be very difficult to make bridge sense out of them. Your first instinct in giving three cards to your partner is to discard what you don't want. This is obviously not what is intended; but what should East and West—playing the first 3–2–1 exchange—do in a case like this?

They start with:

	West		East
	S: A 10 9 8		S: 7 6
	H: 7 6		H: A 10 9 8
	D: J 10 9		D: K Q 3 2
	C: K Q 3 2		C: J 10 9

East gives his partner his two Spades and his Two of Diamonds to show his preferred suit. West passes over his two Hearts and his Two of Clubs as his 'calling' card. Next East gives West the Jack and Ten of Clubs, and receives in return the Jack and Ten of Diamonds. Finally,

East passes over his Nine of Clubs in exchange for West's Nine of Diamonds. The hands they then have to bid on are:

	West		*East*
S:	A 10 9 8 7 6	S:	———————
H:	———————	H:	A 10 9 8 7 6
D:	2	D:	K Q J 10 9 3
C:	K Q J 10 9 3	C:	2

They would have been better off with their original cards, bidding a modest One of whichever minor suit they preferred and leaving the Goulash for another time.

In the end, the first form of Goulash mentioned in 'General Information'—the five-, five-, three-card deal— is the most entertaining, even if you have to agree to the convention mentioned in it: 'In Goulashes *only*, the lead of a King denies the Ace.' In the first place, there is always a chance, not provided by the other two forms, of those 100 points for a misdeal—a penalty which might be profitably introduced into non-Goulash Coarse Bridge some time. Secondly, it nearly always produces a remarkable and surprising set of hands. The sort of hands you read about in the bridge columns as freakish and bizarre are very nearly everyday occurrences in 5–5–3 Goulash, and having the opportunity to play them, even if you do go down in a grand slam, is an exhilarating and cheerful experience.

If we regarded a Goulash as so 'Not Bridge' that we refused to play it, what earthly chance would we ever have had of playing a hand like South's in Seven Clubs— and making them?

```
          S: A K Q J 10 9 8
          H: ——————
          D: 5 4
          C: 7 6 5 4
```

```
S: ——————              N              S: 7 6 5 3
H: K J 10 9 4 3     W      E          H: A 8 7 6
D: K Q J 10 8 7          S             D: 9 6 3 2
C: 3                                   C: 2
```

```
          S: 4 2
          H: Q 5 2
          D: A
          C: A K Q J 10 9 8
```

A couple of nights later another Goulash brightened the end of the evening by producing this hand:

```
          S: A K Q 8 7 6 3 2
          H: ——————————
          D: K J 6
          C: 3 2
```

```
S: 9 5 4                N             S: J 10
H: 9 7 6 5 3 2      W      E          H: ——————
D: ——————                S             D: 10 9 8 7 5 4 3 2
C: 10 9 8 7                            C: 6 5 4
```

```
          S: ——————
          H: A K Q J 10 8 4
          D: A Q
          C: A K Q J
```

Seven No Trumps were bid and made by South—and profitably, since it is one of the lesser known conventions of the Goulash that if one side is vulnerable both sides shall be considered so.

As an academic study both these Goulashes are interesting in that they showed how often, as the experts claim, a void (or chicane) in one hand is matched by a void in another—though rarely, one imagines, by a void in all three other hands, as happened in the great No Trumps hand above.

The truth about the Goulash is that it is worth resorting to when 'normal' play has been bogged down in a number of sterile deals; it is also an entertaining interlude even in a session of normally entertaining Coarse Bridge. And in reckoning up the joys and advantages of Coarse Bridge the continued recognition and encouragement of the strictly illegal Goulash is without question an added asset.

One can only feel sorry for those whose bigotry and literalistic fanaticism does not permit them to join us, but who are condemned to walk through the fields of Life in antiseptic gloves, missing so much and so much.

Reflecting in the final pages of this study on the nature and attraction of Coarse Bridge, its infinite appeal undoubtedly stems from its air of universal friendliness. It is a world open to all, but its conditions of entry are strict, and firmly based on the precepts of Liberty, Equality and Fraternity. Once you are a member of the community you are there for life; there is no known instance of a Coarse Bridge player defecting to any other bridge world, except very briefly to help them out and make a fourth they will certainly live to regret having had to ask for. The player with ambitions in Higher Bridge will never have set foot in the world of Coarse Bridge; he will have instinctively shied away from it and placed his sights right from the beginning on the target of 'bettering' himself.

The world of Coarse Bridge is not a narrow one; all are welcome who qualify and have the temperament to live a life where the Seven Deadly Sins are unknown. Those who would bring Pride or Lechery, Envy or Anger, Covetousness, Gluttony or Sloth to the card table will find themselves excluded. Well, perhaps Sloth can be omitted from the list, for the tempo in the Coarse Bridge world can hardly be regarded as a hectic one, and the Irish maxim that 'the Man who made Time, made plenty of it' is generally accepted.

The Sloth would not cause much comment in surroundings where there are many who, while not inert, are as a rule certainly far from ert.*

The Seven Virtues, on the other hand, flourish naturally and freely in the world of Coarse Bridge, for there you find Faith, Hope and Charity in abundance, as well as Justice, Prudence, Temperance and Fortitude when they are needed—which is often. Above all Coarse Bridge is the world of Tolerance and Liberalism. If you feel inclined one day to amend the present-day scoring system to incorporate features of the one that prevailed in the earliest days of the game, the suggestion that a grand slam should rate 2250 points unvulnerable or vulnerable, as against the penny-pinching modern score of 1000 points unvulnerable and 1500 vulnerable, is likely to be accepted without much opposition.

---

* This neologism is not my own invention. It is derived from a man on the BBC news staff who sounded otherwise educated but reported on the air that a certain part of British industry was suffering 'from lack of ertia'. Credit where credit is due.

The Seven Virtues

As an experiment, that is, because in Coarse Bridge anything will willingly be tried out once. If, in the unlikely event of a grand slam actually being bid at a Coarse Bridge table, there is any objection to the score of 2250 points it will not come from declarer and dummy, but from their opponents. A little short-sightedly, in my view. With 2250 points as the incentive to make a grand slam, the defenders may well have an unexpected number of opportunities to double and so defeat these optimistic contracts and pick up some handsome scores above the line.

Once you have agreed to adopt the 2250 grand slam score, the question of reverting to modern scoring is a matter for frank discussion in depth and eventual compromise—sometimes a little difficult with the table divided 2–2 on the question. But in the end a cut of the cards can decide one way or the other and so get everybody out of the bog that is inevitably created by the frank discussion of anything in depth.

Perhaps the stranger, reading these words on the virtues of Coarse Bridge and those who practise it, may consider that the praise is too fulsome and that we are altogether too smug and priggish even for a contented and expanding band of optimists. But have I really exaggerated? Do we not have good reason to pride ourselves on our honesty and equanimity and our belief that though victory is desirable, it is not to be attained at the cost of human dignity and a sense of values?

There is nothing, I mean, that occurs in Coarse Bridge to approach the cynicism of the following self-explanatory excerpt from a newspaper bridge article. The details of the play are immaterial; the two illustrations tell us all we want to know of 'match play' in Higher Bridge.

At the start of the hand the cards lay as follows:

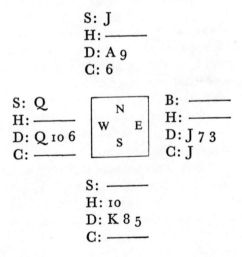

S: J 3 2
H: A Q 5
D: A 9 4
C: K 6 5 4

S: K Q 10 8 7
H: 2
D: Q 10 6
C: J 9 7 2

S: 9 6 5 4
H: 7 6 3
D: J 7 3 2
C: 10 8

S: A
H: K J 10 9 8 4
D: K 8 5
C: A Q 3

The bidding ended with South playing Seven Hearts.
Nine tricks later the hands looked like this:

S: J
H: ———
D: A 9
C: 6

S: Q
H: ———
D: Q 10 6
C: ———

B: ———
H: ———
D: J 7 3
C: J

S: ———
H: 10
D: K 8 5
C: ———

How, may one ask, did West's Jack of Clubs get into East's hand? Passed under the table, perhaps? In Coarse Bridge there is considerable freedom of action, one way and another, but we have certainly never resorted to exchanging cards under the table.

It was subsequently pointed out to me that the diagram with the Jack of Clubs in East's hand was only to illustrate what South *thought* East had got. A likely story! No smoke without fire, I've always said. When everybody is busy developing systems of silent bidding by smoke signals and semaphore that make the American Indian and the tic-tac man on an English racecourse look like helpless inarticulates they can hardly expect us to believe that the Jack in East's hand was only in South's imagination. The bridge columns deal with hard facts of life, not dreams—like the newspapers they are printed in. Small wonder the article was headed 'Difficult Road to a Grand Slam'. But enough of other kinds of bridge and their suspect ways.

Many pleasant things about Coarse Bridge will have emerged, I hope, in the course of this study. And high among them is surely the strictly amateur spirit, in the best sense, of what was never intended to be more than a pastime. Skill, luck, quick-wittedness and hopeless ineptitude all play their part in the game, but skill is not boasted about, luck is not envied, quick-wittedness is not resented, nor hopeless ineptitude despised.

We do not keep a note of winnings and losses in a diary, to be reckoned up like a balance-sheet at the end of the year. Whom would we hope to impress if we did? Ourselves? Impossible. Our playmates? Improbable. Such book-keepers do not belong to our world, for their way lie the ambitions, the obsessions and the frustrations of the player who, consciously or unconsciously, wishes he could be a professional, but is just not good enough.

The final joy of Coarse Bridge is that there is nowhere to go from here. No one is promoted; no one is demoted. There are no such things as higher or lower circles of Coarse Bridge. Few people leave Coarse Bridge, and with the arrival on the scene of an ever-increasing number of new young players one's playing circle is healthily and picturesquely extended every year.

There is no such thing as a Generation Gap; we mingle and share our problems freely and with understanding. Gerry has had trouble for decades over what to bid when she has 'real' Diamonds in her hand and wants to support her partner's strong opening Two Clubs; Bill and Brian and Victoria, all newly arrived, have the same difficulty.

Situations do not change, and yet they are always altering circumstances; conditions, ethics, customs, rules and regulations are not tampered with, but their nature is flexible. Laws revised by Ruling Bodies are generally ignored, although we may adopt some of them if they happen to suit us, but on the whole we tend to believe that there are already enough Laws to give us a trouble-free game of cards. More of them would baffle us and disturb the Elysian air of our tables.

Even in the world of Higher Bridge, where conventions are invented between one deal and the next, where international championships lead to international antagonism, to acrimony and wounded feelings, huffiness and ill-will, contests come to an end, never to be renewed—because the competitors have walked out and the tension is unbearable. But Coarse Bridge, like the Last Rubber itself, goes on for ever.

As one of the earliest bridge correspondents put it,

differing slightly from Masefield: 'We shall not all sleep, but we shall all be changed, in a moment, in the twinkling of an eye, at the last trump.'

Ringmer,
Sussex

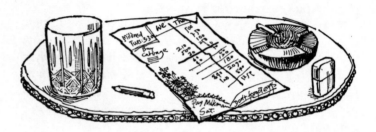

Glossary of terms used in Coarse Bridge

(Glossary: list and explanations of abstruse, obsolete, dialect or technical terms)—*Con. Oxf. Dict.*

Above the line: The place on the score-card where They score the tricks We didn't make, and We put the overtricks They did.

Auction: The period preceding the actual play, when Special Announcements and Counter-announcements are made, and Hopes are publicly expressed.

Auction Bridge: A game with some rules that might well be applied to Coarse Bridge (see page 55), and not to be despised.

Below the line: The place on Their score card which needs very careful watching, as They are very inclined to include in it points which don't belong there. Also the place very rarely looked at by our partner when We are bidding.

Bid: Something you say when you shouldn't.

Business double: A double that means you *hope* to put your opponents down a trick or two. See *Redouble.*

Call: A term that embraces all bids, doubles, redoubles and passes; also comment and expletives.

Cash: A rather vulgar phrase to describe playing your one winning card as soon as possible.

Chicane: An old term, now being revived, for a void or blank suit. Etymologically related to chicanery, so caution is advised. The *Con. Oxf. Dict.* defines the term as 'hand without any trumps in bridge'. Odd bridge they play at Oxf.

Contract: The mess your bidding has landed you in. There is unfortunately no facility, even in Coarse Bridge, to contract out, although it is understood some research is being made into the possibilities of this.

Contract lenses: Glasses your partner should put on to study the score before jumping to Five Clubs when only Two are needed for game.

Convention: An agreement between partners that what they bid does, does not, might, or ought to mean what you (and They) think it does. Conventions may be agreed upon, explained and discussed before, during, or after a hand; also, by common consent, in mid-trick.

Cross-ruffing: A highly fancy procedure, hard to come by.

Cue bid: A bid that means when you say Four Clubs you haven't necessarily got any, but would like to hear your partner reply Four Spades so that you, like the mug you are, can go Six Hearts.

Deal: The act of distributing the cards to the players. Has sometimes been known to interrupt, and even bring to an end, conversation about the previous hand.

Declarer: A player who has committed himself to playing the hand before he has any idea what dummy looks like.

Defender: A player who has to play against the Declarer; also his own partner.

Discard: The card you should have kept back.

Double: An ambiguous term addressed to your opponents when you think you can put them down, and to your partner when you want to know whether he thinks he can.

Double jump: See *Jump bid.*

Doubleton: Typically coy baby-talk bridge expression. 'Singleton' means an only child; 'doubleton' means two children.

Duck (v.i): Deliberately losing a trick when you could win it. Great courage is needed for this and it is rarely found in Coarse Bridge.

False card: The loser you play without thinking, but whose significance is taken very seriously by your partner and opponents.

Finesse: Trying to take a trick with a card that is not the highest in its suit. Its success depends entirely on your opponents playing correctly—that is, not taking the trick when they could easily. Rarely encountered in Coarse Bridge.

Finessing against partner: An unconscious action noticed only by partner finessed against, if then. For a map of this campaign, see page 67.

Forcing bid: A Strong Two, like Two Clubs, which immediately sets everybody at the table discussing what the negative response is, what you should have in your hand for a positive response and what does the Blackwood 4–5 No Trumps mean please?

Free double: A double that doesn't do anybody any harm but might move your partner to open his mouth just once.

Game: A game is won by the side that gets 100 points below the line. Rarely achieved in the first six months of playing Coarse Bridge, except by your opponents.

Honours: Ace, King, Queen, Jack, Ten of the same suit. Four of them in a suit contract produce 100 points, five of them 150. Four Aces in No Trumps score 150 points. Often considered sufficient reason for bidding more than you should and ample consolation for going down 300.

Jump bid: Sometimes known as *double jump*. It is a bid that has to be made loud and clear, and if necessary repeated *fortissimo*, to ensure that your somnolent partner knows what you're doing.

Lead: The most difficult moment in any Coarse Bridge player's life. It occurs numberless times every evening and never gets any less difficult.

Loser: The player who wins least money in the evening. Also, a card in your hand without a future.

Overtake: A daring and unorthodox taking of your partner's trick. The positive response to this convention is: 'Did you mean to do that?'

Over-tricks: The tricks you ought to have bid, but didn't.

Part score: Odd figures found below the line on the score-card. Rarely consulted.

Pass: The privilege of silence, seldom taken advantage of.

Penalty card: Unknown in Coarse Bridge.

Penalty double: Posh name for business double.

Point count: A complicated form of mental arithmetic which tells you, without your knowing it, how many Quick Tricks you have.

Psychic bid: A bid made on the principle that our guess is as good as theirs, probably better.

Redouble: Your opponents' inevitable reaction to your double of their final bid.

Rubber, the final: Begins shortly before midnight; usually takes two and a half hours to finish.

Singleton: A promising card but rendered useless by declarer drawing trumps.

Slam, Grand: What we ought to have bid, but didn't.

Slam, Small: What we ought never to have bid, but did.

Trump (n., and v.t.): The things (nn.) you always forget to draw until your opponents begin to trump (v.t.) some of your best cards.

Vulnerable: A term describing a purely technical state of having won a game. Rarely noted or acted on in Coarse Bridge.

Yarborough: Any hand not actually stuffed with Aces and Kings. Often referred to as *an absolute Yarborough.*

Bibliography

Below are listed a few of the works which will help the reader to improve his game, and extend his knowledge of the historical background, philosophy and social significance of Coarse Bridge.

The Art of Coarse Cricket by Spike Hughes
The Art of Coarse Gardening by Spike Hughes
The Art of Coarse Cookery by Spike Hughes
The Art of Coarse Entertaining by Spike Hughes
The Art of Coarse Language by Spike Hughes

FOR THE COARSE BRIDGE HOSTESS

Cold Dishes for All Seasons by Charmian and Spike Hughes